A Step-by-Step Guide to Wills and Probate

by

A K Biggs,
Probate Consultant and formerly the Registrar of the
Winchester District Probate Registry

and

K Donnelly,
Manager of the Probate Department of the Principal Registry
of the Family Division

Fourth Edition

London
Callow Publishing
2008

ISBN 978 1 898899 98 3

First published 1991
Second edition, 1994
Third edition, 2000
Fourth edition, 2008

Every care is taken in the preparation of this publication, but the
authors and the publisher cannot accept responsibility for the
consequences of any error, however caused.

© 1984 – 2008, A K Biggs, K Donnelly
Published by Callow Publishing Limited,
PO Box 56245, London N4 2TD
www.callowpublishing.com
Printed and bound in Great Britain by MPG Books Ltd, Bodmin,
Cornwall.

Preface

Everyone should write a will. In Chapter 1 of *A Step-by-Step Guide to Wills and Probate*, we say why, and explain how to write a simple will. Other events relating to a will after it has been made are also dealt with.

Later chapters are devoted to sorting out the affairs of someone who has died. This involves applying to a probate registry (which is a court of law) for a "grant of representation". The application is made by the deceased person's proposed personal representative. The personal representative may be an executor appointed by a will. Alternatively, the personal representative may be an administrator if the deceased did not appoint an executor by will or the executor has died or is unable to act, or the deceased died without making a valid will. There may be more than one personal representative. The grant is the formal document which establishes the validity of the will if there is one, and gives the personal representative full authority to deal with the deceased's affairs.

The personal representative has to identify and value all the deceased's property before applying for the grant. The value of the property determines whether or not a fee is charged by the probate registry, and whether or not inheritance tax has to be paid.

Once the grant has been issued, the probate court is no longer involved and it is up to the personal representative to collect together all the property and ensure that it is correctly divided among those who should receive it. There are rules about who inherits the property of someone who leaves no will.

Clearly, a short book of this kind cannot be comprehensive. There are many times when we point out possible pitfalls and suggest that it would be wise to consult a solicitor. Inheritance tax, for example, can be complicated and it is beyond the scope of this book to go into any detail about planning to reduce tax liability. The Chancellor of the Exchequer's budget statement of October 2007 assisted in reducing the tax burden on married couples and civil partners. Likewise, trusts are usually complex, and this is another matter where we think a solicitor is almost certainly necessary.

We have avoided legal jargon as far as possible, but some special terms cannot be avoided. They are explained in the text. In addition, there is a glossary on page 155, for quick reference.

The information given in this book applies to England and Wales only. The law in other parts of the United Kingdom and Europe is quite different, and is not covered here.

The book does not deal with what was sometimes called a "living will" whereby the person who made it set out what was to happen in the event of life-threatening illness. This form of "will" is now provided for by way of a lasting power of attorney made under the Mental Capacity Act 2005.

The book contains examples of certain of the forms used. The forms on pages 127 to 129 are reproduced with the kind permission of The Solicitors' Law Stationery Society Limited. The remaining forms Crown copyright and are reproduced pursuant to the Crown copyright waiver.

A K Biggs
K Donnelly
April 2008

Contents

Chapter 1

Making Your Will

Why Make a Will?

There are several excellent reasons for making a will. The most important is that it means your property will go to the people you decide should have it. Your home, money, shares and other personal belongings can be used to provide for family and close friends. Those who make no will have little or no control over what happens to their property after death, with the result that distant or disliked relations, or even the Crown, may benefit from their lack of foresight. This is because the law provides that when a person dies without leaving a will, certain portions of the person's estate are reserved to members of the family. These reserved portions – called "statutory legacies" – are paid to close relatives; anything left after that could go to more distant relations.

Another good reason for making a will is that it helps those who are left behind to cope. They know what was intended and how to deal with the deceased person's possessions.

When making a will, you may appoint almost anyone to sort out your affairs after your death. This person is called an "executor". Women executors are sometimes called "executrixes". Your executor can be a relative, a trusted friend or a professional person such as a solicitor or an accountant. Professional people appointed as executors usually charge for these services. You may have more than one executor.

A will may be as simple or as complicated as desired. It may contain a single gift of all property to one person, or many gifts to different people. Trusts may be created in a will. These include arrangements for making a gift on the happening of a certain event, such as an eighteenth birthday or marriage. A trust may also be set up to provide for more than one generation – often for grandchildren and great grandchildren. Gifts to charity may be made, and guardians for young children may be appointed.

If you own property abroad, you should bear in mind that a will which is valid in England and Wales may not be valid to dispose of your foreign assets. To deal with property in another country, it may be necessary to make a will in accordance with the law of that country. If so, professional advice from a solicitor is essential.

A person making a will is called a "testator" if a man, or a "testatrix" if a woman. A person who has made a will dies "testate", and one who has not, dies "intestate".

A will has no effect until the death of the person who made it.

How to Make a Will

The law of England and Wales requires a will to be in writing. This means it must be handwritten, typewritten or printed by a word processor. A will made by video, for example, is not valid. There is an exception to the rule about the will being written which applies in very limited circumstances – see page 22. A will can be written on any piece of paper and, provided the formalities are complied with, the document is perfectly valid, just as if a solicitor had prepared it. A point which recurs throughout this chapter is that it is unwise to try to make a will "sound legal". Plain words plainly expressed are best. Otherwise, you run the risk that the effect you achieve will be quite different from what you intended.

If you decide to make your will yourself, you can buy a will form. There are many types available and most stationers stock them. They come with instructions about the procedures to follow.

Printed will forms are used mainly by people who wish to make straightforward gifts of their property. For anything complicated, professional help should be sought, unless you are absolutely confident about what you are doing; even then, think carefully before doing it yourself. It is not only people with plenty of money who need to go to a solicitor. In fact, most incorrect wills are made without professional advice by people who have quite small amounts of property.

There are many organisations other than solicitors and banks offering will-making services, including via the internet. The quality of service provided by these will-drafting companies, in terms of the level of legal expertise, varies. It is worth remembering that as yet no government has legislated to require affiliation to a governing body, or to set a minimum standard of legal knowledge, before anyone can become a will draftsman. Nevertheless, many "independent" will drafters do provide a good service. The difficulty is to determine who is competent and who is not. It is a choice for you to make as a testator. The editors advise that if you intend to make a simple will this can be done personally but, if your property is of a value that you require advice about tax planning, trusts, lifetime or deferred gifts, then it is advisable to seek advice from someone suitably qualified.

The rest of this chapter is devoted to appointing your executors; working out how to express the gifts you wish to make in your will; and meeting the legal requirements to ensure your will is valid.

Drafting a Will

Obviously, the will must be drafted first, and the document then written, typed or printed. Do not make your will "sound legal" by using words which seem legalistic or technical. More mistakes are made on this point than on any other. Wills are interpreted by the courts with the widest possible tolerance and always with the purpose of giving effect to the testator's or testatrix's wishes, but sometimes it is impossible to discover exactly what was intended. If there is any ambiguity in the contents of a will, there may be trouble later.

There are, though, certain legal terms which we cannot avoid using in this book. They have precise meanings and the glossary on pages 155–157 gives brief explanations. It may be worthwhile reading the glossary at this point, as well as referring to it when appropriate.

The best plan is to draft your will in rough, and satisfy yourself that it is absolutely clear and not capable of being interpreted differently from how you intend. Ask someone else to read it, just to make sure. Use plain and straightforward language. If you are in any doubt, consult a solicitor. If you wish to set up a trust or arrange for a life interest or deferred gift (see page 11) it must be done properly. If you have confidence in your own abilities, all well and good. Otherwise, a visit to a solicitor will be worthwhile.

In the paragraphs which follow, there are examples of the provisions found in most wills, and at the end of the chapter there are examples of complete wills. This chapter is a guide to making a simple will only. Anything complicated, and it is wise to consult a solicitor.

Structure of a Will

The will should open with introductory words such as "This is the last will of me, John Arthur Brown, of 49 Acacia Gardens Middlemarch Loamshire LO77 7JX". There should then be a clause revoking any former will (see page 26). The will should then go on to appoint executors, to make gifts of particular items or general legacies (gifts of money) and to make a gift of "residue". There may be other special provisions. When all the gifts have been set out, the attestation clause is added.

All these matters are considered in the paragraphs which follow.

Appointing the Executors

It has already been noted that an executor is the person named in a will who is to be responsible for dealing with the testator's or testatrix's affairs after death. There may be more than one executor, but no more than four can act in the administration of the estate at any one time. It will be their task to implement the provisions of the will, although when the time comes they may employ a solicitor to do it for them.

It is usual to select as executor a relative, close friend or professional adviser. It is wise to talk to your proposed executor(s) first, to make sure they are able and willing to be appointed. It is also sensible, if appointing an individual, to choose someone younger, who is likely to survive the person making the will.

Executors have special powers given to them by the will. Upon death, they can deal with the property immediately. They do not have to wait for the formalities (see Chapter 6) to be completed. Instead, the will itself gives them the authority to handle the deceased person's affairs.

An executor can decide how the deceased's body is be disposed of, even if there is a family dispute, and may override the family's wishes. The duties of executors are explained in detail in Chapter 7.

Below are examples of typical clauses appointing executors.

> "I appoint Frederick Joseph Bloggs of 379 Sycamore Drive, Middlemarch, Loamshire MD8 4BP and Andrew Leonard Smith of 57 Flowerpot Way, Middlemarch, Loamshire MD9 4BP to be my executors."

It is always better to appoint more than one executor in case, when it comes to proving the will, one of the persons named declines to act as executor or has died.

> "I appoint Mary Anne Brown of 54 Honeypot Lane, Middlemarch, Loamshire MD7 3BP to be my sole executrix. If she shall not survive me by thirty days, I appoint Frederick Joseph Bloggs of 379 Sycamore Drive, Middlemarch, Loamshire MD8 4BP and Andrew Leonard Smith of 57 Flowerpot Way, Middlemarch, Loamshire MD9 4BP to be my executors."

This type of appointment is often made along with a gift of all property to the sole executor or executrix, usually where a husband or wife or civil partner is leaving everything to the other spouse or partner.

> "I appoint the Black Eagle Bank to be my sole executor which may act upon its standard terms and conditions in force at my death."

Appointing a bank or similar type of corporation has advantages over appointing an individual. If an individual is appointed, he or she might die before the testator, or for some other reason not be able to act as executor when the time comes. This cannot happen if a corporation is selected. Even if the bank or company merges or amalgamates with another, arrangements will be made to cover existing appointments as executor contained in wills. It is sensible to check with the company before appointing it executor in case a special wording is required, or in case its constitution prevents it from acting as an executor. And it is worth remembering that the company can renounce probate (that is, decline to act as an executor – see page 42) in the same way as any other executor can. You should also find out the company's charges before appointing it your executor, although these charges will be paid out of the estate.

> "I appoint the equity partners or members as appropriate, at the date of my death, in the firm of James Robinson and Ellis (or the firm which has succeeded to and carries on its practice) to be my executors."

This type of wording is used when a firm of solicitors or other type of partnership firm is appointed executor. It is not very likely that you will in fact use this form of words if writing your own will; if you intend to appoint solicitors as your executors, they would probably be drafting the will for you. But this kind of appointment is common, so it is mentioned here for the sake of completeness. To be a valid appointment, all the equity partners in a firm must be appointed, although not more than four such partners can act as executors at any one time.

To ensure that the appointment of executors would remain effective after any merger or amalgamation of the firm, the words about successors are included.

It is stressed that the above examples are only some of the types of appointment which can be made, but they are the most common.

Appointing Guardians for Children

A person who has a child or children under eighteen may wish to appoint a guardian who would care for the children if one or both parents should die while the children are still young. This is a complicated matter. For example, under the Children Act 1989, the parent who survives would almost certainly have what is called "parental responsibility" for the children and so be entitled to care for them in preference to anyone named in the will of the parent who dies. It is usual to make the appointment operative only on the death of both parents. Anyone planning to appoint a guardian for children should consult a solicitor, rather than attempt to write his or her own will.

Specific Gifts

It is commonly thought that all the testator's or testatrix's belongings must be itemised and disposed of individually. In fact, that is not the case, as will be seen later in this chapter, but "specific gifts" of particular items are an important part of any will. Before committing anything to writing it is sensible to make a list of your belongings and marshal your thoughts. Someone to whom you would like to leave a gift may have expressed a wish for, or admired, some particular article. There may be other special reasons for leaving certain items to certain people. There may be a charity you would like to help.

What follows are examples of most forms of gift. They are deliberately general and should be adapted to your particular needs, bearing in mind that you should express your gift as precisely as possible.

> "I leave my crystal decanter to my friend Henry Robert Smith of 15 Acacia Road, London NE4 9XY."

This is the simplest type of "bequest" (an alternative name for a gift when the gift is of goods rather than land or a house), but it illustrates the critical factors. It identifies clearly both the gift and the person to whom it is to be given. This is important, as any ambiguity may cause trouble when your property comes to be distributed. Nothing is worse than a quarrel over gifts in a will. Obviously, if the testator in this example has more than one crystal decanter, more words would be needed to identify which decanter Henry is to have, for example, "my Waterford crystal whisky decanter".

> "I leave the total sum (including any interest accrued to the date of my death) standing in my account with the Black Eagle Bank to Joseph Arthur Bloggs of 109 Strawberry Fields, London NE79 1JZ."

This type of wording can be used in connection with any bank or savings account. It identifies the account, deals with the whole of the sum and the interest, and makes it absolutely clear who is to have the money. The drawback is that if the testator closes this particular bank account after making his will, Mr Bloggs loses the gift even though another account may have been opened at another bank. But as long as there is an account with the named bank at the date of death – it may be the one which existed when the will was made, or one which was opened later – Mr Bloggs will receive the gift. The point is that the will deals with the property at the date of death, not the date of making the will.

To cover the possibility that the person making the will may move the account to another bank, the following words can be added:

> "If I no longer have an account with the Black Eagle Bank at the date of my death, I leave the total sum (including interest as aforesaid) in any other bank account I may then have to Joseph Arthur Bloggs of 109 Strawberry Fields, London NE79 1JZ."

This will deal with the possibility that you may close the particular account, but still wish Mr Bloggs to have the contents of a replacement bank account. It could, on the other hand, mean that the beneficiary will receive more than was intended. This could happen, for example, if Mr Bloggs ends up being entitled to the balance in an account which is an amalgamation of two or more accounts. This may be acceptable, or you may wish to avoid it. The choice is yours, but you must be clear and unambiguous. People who have several bank accounts may need to identify them by the account numbers.

So far, we have dealt with straightforward gifts of personal property (that is, property other than land, houses etc). There are many ways of making gifts of land or houses in a will, but the basic rule applies; the gift and the recipient should be clearly identified. For example:

> "I leave my house, 13 Acacia Avenue, Middlemarch, Loamshire MD3 4JX to Mary Elizabeth Jones of 17 Coronation Grove, Eastbury, Loamshire EA9 2ZX."

All these gifts have in common that the property and the beneficiaries are clearly identified. This is so whether the gift is of personal property (as in the first two examples – the decanter and the money in the bank), or real property (as in this example – the house). The gift, or "devise", of the house above is simply set out and can leave no room for doubt. As with the money in the bank, the wording can be altered to take account of any changes after making the will. For example:

> "If I no longer own 13 Acacia Avenue at the date of my death, I leave the freehold or leasehold property which I own at that date to Mary Elizabeth Jones of 17 Coronation Grove, Eastbury, Loamshire EA9 2ZX."

This should ensure that Ms Jones receives your house, but again there are drawbacks. For example, you may acquire a second house before you die. You may wish to leave the second house also to the fortunate Ms Jones, or you may decide that someone else should have it. The answer to this and to other problems is to make a codicil; this is explained on page 28.

One of the most common errors in wording a gift is the gift of the motor car. "I give to Charlie Briggs my Rolls Royce motor car" is fine as long as the testator or testatrix owns such a car at the date of death. But if he sells the Rolls Royce and buys a Porsche, the gift fails. On the other hand, "I give to Charlie Briggs my Rolls Royce motor car or such other car as is in my possession at the date of my death" means Charlie will receive any car owned.

It must be borne in mind that a specific gift fails if the property which is the subject of the gift no longer belongs to the testator or testatrix at death, unless there is a "saving clause", such as those set out above, which substitute another piece of property. Without such a clause, Ms Jones will not receive the house, and Charlie will not be driving the Rolls Royce, if the testator sells it after making the will.

Sometimes testators put conditions on their gifts. The most common type requires the recipient to survive the testator by a specified number of days. For example:

"I leave the sum of £100 to Helen Jane Troy of 15 Leigh Gardens, Middlemarch, Loamshire MD1 7FG provided she survives me by 30 days."

The period of time for survival is a matter of choice, but it is a good idea not to make it too long; anything over thirty days or so may cause difficulties, to both the executor and the beneficiary.

The survival clause can be added to any type of specific gift and to the appointment of executors (see page 4). There is one point to bear in mind – the actual passage of days is calculated from the day following the date of death.

"I leave the sum of £100 to Helen Jane Troy of 15 Leigh Gardens, Middlemarch, Loamshire MD1 7FG provided she survives me by 30 days. If she does not so survive me, I leave the said sum of £100 to Mary Elizabeth Jardine of 17 Garden Road, Acaciaville, Loamshire AC9 7TB."

Quite often, the testator does not wish a specific gift to fail altogether if the beneficiary dies before the testator. It is possible, as shown in the example immediately above, to provide that if the proposed beneficiary dies before the testator, the gift which would have been his or hers passes to someone else. This is quite often coupled with a survival clause, as in our example, which provides for the gift to be made to someone else if the first person does not survive by the required number of days. The reason for a provision like this is to avoid the property being transferred twice – once to Helen and then again from her to someone else – within a short time. So, if Helen dies before the testator, or if she survives him but then dies within thirty days after the testator's death, the gift goes to Mary. To be technical, Mary is a "substituted beneficiary" and the gift to her is a "substituted gift".

There is one type of specific gift which is not made void by the death of the beneficiary before the testator. The Wills Act 1837, which, although it has been amended over the years, remains in force today, contains a special provision relating to gifts to children and "issue". The words "child" and "issue" do mean different things here. "Children" means sons and/or daughters of the testator; "issue" means children and grandchildren, great grandchildren and so on. The Act (section 33) provides that a gift to a child who dies in the testator's lifetime will pass to the issue of that child (unless the will states otherwise). This has the same effect as providing in a will for an alternative beneficiary. It must be stressed that this provision applies to gifts to children only. It is intended as a last resort to cover a will which has become out of date and there is a danger that the estate will not be distributed as the testator would have wished. While it is helpful to know of this statutory rule, it should not be relied upon in substitution for making full provision in a will. It is also worth remembering that "children" includes any child adopted by the testator.

> "I leave the sum of £10,000 to Christopher John Reynolds of 17 Acacia Road, Middlemarch, Loamshire MD99 2JK upon his attaining the age of eighteen years and I direct that the whole of the income from this sum be applied for the benefit of the said Christopher John Reynolds until he shall attain the age of eighteen years."

It is quite usual to make conditions controlling the manner in which a gift is to be paid, or the time at which it is to be paid. You may wish to have payment deferred until a beneficiary reaches a certain age or marries. This is achieved by using words such as those above. The first part of the gift sets out the sum (£10,000) and the contingency – Christopher reaching the age of eighteen. The last part directs that Christopher is to receive the income from the capital sum up to his eighteenth birthday. The legal consequence of this is that the gift has effect immediately on the testator's death, even though Christopher may not have possession of the capital sum if he is still under eighteen when the testator dies. Complicated as it is, this is the simplest way of making a deferred or limited gift. The will would have to go on to appoint a trustee (see below) to take care of the money until Christopher's eighteenth birthday. Clearly, this type of bequest must be worded very carefully if it is to succeed, and legal advice should be sought if it is contemplated.

Property can be left in trust – that is, it can be placed in the care of a trustee who manages it for the benefit of the eventual recipient. This would be appropriate where the beneficiary is a child. Another possibility is that property may be left to someone for a limited period of time – usually for life. For example, a married person might leave property to his or her spouse for the spouse's lifetime, with a provision that it then goes to the children. These are both complex subjects and if you need to make a bequest or devise in these terms, you should consult a solicitor. This advice appears often in this book, but to illustrate the point, consider the following examples:

(1) "I leave all my property to my son Frederick Joseph Bloggs and, in the event of his death, I leave everything to my daughter-in-law."

(2) "I leave my freehold property 17 Acacia Avenue to my wife Helen Jane Troy in trust for her life. After the death of my wife, I leave the said property to our family."

(3) "I leave all my insurance policies to my daughter Judith Carol Troy in trust for her children. If my daughter should die, the said policies are to be held in trust by her husband Wayne Gary Troy until his death when they are to be shared by their relatives."

All these gifts may seem clear, but they fail to state the testator's intentions with sufficient precision to enable the terms of the will to be carried out. For example, in (1), which daughter-in-law is meant – Frederick's wife, or the wife of another son? In (2), what does "our family" mean – are cousins included? Are aunts and uncles included? In (3), if which daughter should die – Judith, or another? Who are their "relatives"?

To summarise:

- All specific gifts should be expressed in terms making it clear what property is being given and what person is to receive it.
- It is possible to make provision for the gift to be saved in case the recipient dies before the testator. If a gift does fail, the sum of money or item given becomes part of the "residue" of the estate and is distributed in accordance with the directions concerning residue given in the will (see below).
- Gifts can be immediate, taking effect on the death of the testator; or they can be deferred (for example, until the recipient attains a certain age). Gifts can be for the benefit of the immediate recipient or of a third party, the immediate recipient merely acting as a trustee.
- Gifts can be expressed to be for life only, in which case the gift is called a beneficial interest. When the person given the beneficial interest dies, the gift passes to another named person or persons.
- If you are in any doubt at all about the way in which you wish your gifts to be worded, consult a solicitor. This applies both to specific and residuary gifts, especially if you wish to make special provisions to set up a trust or trusts.

Gift of Residue

As mentioned on page 6, it is a common error to suppose that all property must be disposed of by name or description. It is unlikely that that would be possible in any event since a person writing a will today cannot know what possessions he or she will have at death, which may be many years ahead. As has been noted already, a will does not take effect until the death of the testator. It may need to be rewritten or amended by codicil (see page 28) from time to time to keep up with changing circumstances, but it should be complete when you make it. In order to do this, it should contain not only specific gifts, but also a "sweeping up" clause which disposes of everything else. This is called a gift, or disposition, of residue.

The straightforward way to make a gift of residue is by a clause such as:

> "I leave the remainder of my estate, both real and personal, to Frederick Joseph Bloggs of 379 Sycamore Drive, Middlemarch, Loamshire LO9 5XQ."

This is a simple gift of all the property (or "estate") which was not disposed of specifically, or which was disposed of but for some reason the disposition has failed. It is most important that a residuary gift be included in a will because it is a way of ensuring that you have control over the ultimate destination of your estate. Any estate not so disposed of is called, unsurprisingly, "undisposed of estate". The full implications of this are discussed on page 15.

Any variation of the basic type of clause, as in the example above, is usually for further defining the wishes of the testator or testatrix. The following examples illustrate this:

To leave all your estate to one person:

> "I leave the whole of my estate, both real and personal, to Frederick Joseph Bloggs of 379 Sycamore Drive, Middlemarch, Loamshire LO9 5XQ."

This gift is still one of residue, despite the fact that there is no other gift.

To leave the remainder of your estate to your children:

> "I leave the remainder of my estate, both real and personal, to my children Carol Frances Jameson, Joanne Louise Jameson and Henry Robert Jameson in equal shares."

This clause can be modified to provide for the death of any of the residuary beneficiaries by adding the words:

> "If any of my said children should predecease me [or 'shall not survive me by x days'] the share which would have gone to that child shall be divided between the survivors in equal shares or if only one child shall survive to that child absolutely."

You will see that there are certain similarities between the wording used in specific gifts and that used in residuary gifts. The points about simplicity and clarity mentioned above in respect of specific gifts apply equally to gifts of residue, and as long as they are kept in mind, there should be little difficulty.

You can dispose of the residue of your estate in any proportions you wish, For example:

"I leave the remainder of my estate, both real and personal, to the following persons in the following percentages:

(i) 50 per cent to Frederick Joseph Bloggs of 12 Loam Hill, Middlemarch, Loamshire MD6 9YS;

(ii) 25 per cent to Mary Ann Bloggs also of 12 Loam Hill, Middlemarch, Loamshire MD6 9YS;

(iii) 15 per cent to Jennifer Felicity Smithe-Tomlinson of The Meadows, Middlemarch, Loamshire MD4 3JP;

(iv) 10 per cent to Robert Macintosh of 79 Loam Heights, Middlemarch, Loamshire MD8 3GY."

This example illustrates how flexible you can make the terms of your will and how much control you have over the way in which your estate is distributed.

Errors of arithmetic are by no means unknown, so if you decide to adopt a formula like this, do double check the addition.

Residue can be left as an absolute gift (as in the examples above), or in a limited way to provide a gift for life, or in trust for the benefit of, say, a child. Gifts of this kind were discussed on pages 10–11.

It is quite common to appoint your executors to be your trustees, in which case the residue is left to them "upon trust". This means that they not only have authority under the will, as executors, to deal with your property immediately after death, but they have a longer term responsibility to take care of the property put into trust. This continues until the trust is wound up and the assets transferred to the ultimate beneficiary or beneficiaries.

The purpose of a gift of the residue of the estate is to ensure, as far as possible, that all your estate is disposed of in the manner you wish. Usually, the recipient of the residue receives most of the estate. This is so whether the gift of residue is to an individual or several persons. We have seen that a will takes effect at the date of death, and that when writing a will a testator or testatrix does not necessarily know what property he or she will have at death. Care is therefore needed to ensure that the person you select as your main beneficiary will in fact receive most of the estate. This can be done by making only small specific gifts and leaving the bulk of the estate to your main beneficiary by way of a gift of residue. Alternatively, you may make a large specific gift to the main beneficiary. The residue is what is left after all the debts and specific legacies have been paid, and if there is nothing left, that is what your residuary beneficiary will get.

To sum up, every will should dispose of the whole of the estate. This can be achieved with any degree of certainty only if there is a gift of residue of the estate.

Estate not Disposed of by the Will

You might think "estate not disposed of" refers to the pictures on the sitting room wall and the premium bonds which were not left to anyone in particular. These small items can form part of the undisposed estate, but the fact that they are not specifically mentioned in the will does not necessarily mean that they count as undisposed of estate under the will. They may instead be part of the residuary estate, which has just been discussed. "Undisposed of estate" means that estate which is not disposed of by the will either by way of a specific gift or under a residuary gift.

The most obvious way to fail to make a gift of residue is to omit to mention the remainder of your estate in your will. It was explained on pages 12–13 that if there is no final sweeping up clause, it is likely that part of the estate will be undisposed of. The less obviously easy way in which to make no residuary gift is to word your residuary clause so that you do not provide for the possibility that one or all of your residuary beneficiaries will die before you. If this happens, that person's share of the residuary estate will be undisposed of.

It has been emphasised that you have the choice about how your estate will be distributed. That is one of the main reasons for making a will. If you do not make a successful gift of the residue, your wishes may be thwarted. By law, undisposed of estate is distributed to those who would be entitled to your estate if you had not made a will at all. Persons who die without having made a will are said to die "intestate" and the laws of intestacy determine how their estates are distributed. Although the way of sharing property under these laws looks fairly straightforward, it is not all it seems and it is quite likely that the people who would benefit may not be those you would have chosen. They could even be people you do not know. The question of entitlement on intestacy is dealt with in Chapter 8.

Gifts to Charities

A gift to a charity is an excellent provision in any will. It has many advantages, not least that it does not attract inheritance tax (see Chapter 4). The greatest advantage, however, and one which is unique to charitable gifts, is that no matter how badly worded the gift, and even if at the date of death the named charity has ceased to exist, the gift cannot fail. Eventually, the sum of money specified in the will as the charitable gift will be paid over for charitable purposes. If necessary, the Attorney General has authority to intervene and select a suitable charity so that the charitable intention is fulfilled.

But it is always better to be safe than sorry and if words such as the following are used there should be little difficulty:

"I give the sum of £100 to the Society for the Preservation of Ancient Civil Servants and declare that the receipt of the treasurer or other authorised officer of the Society shall be sufficient discharge for my executors."

Validity of a Will

We turn next to the formalities which make a will valid. We have already noted that it must be in writing. It must also be properly signed and witnessed. After the death of the testator or testatrix, the will must be "proved" before it can come fully into effect. This involves applying to the probate court and satisfying the court that the will is valid in all respects. The process is described fully in Chapter 6. It is sufficient here to note that all wills are scrutinised to ensure they are in order.

In England and Wales the most important piece of legislation governing how wills are made is the Wills Act 1837. Before that date, practically anything was acceptable as a way to leave money or other personal property; it did not even have to be written down. This was a totally unsatisfactory state of affairs.

The 1837 Act still applies today, and although it has been amended slightly, it has survived almost unaltered. For something to have lasted so long is a good indication that it works well. The validity of a will is decided by the terms of the Act – any deviation and there is a good chance that the will may not be proved. A will is a formal document and the formalities must be followed.

Signing a Will

Let us assume that you have written, typed or word processed the will, there are no mistakes or alterations and you are ready to sign the will and have it witnessed. The correct expression for this is "execution", which may sound sinister but it is the proper term,

It may seem a simple matter to sign a will but it is surprising how many are rejected because of the inadequacy of the testator's signature.

The will must be signed by the person making it ("the testator" or "testatrix"), or by someone at his or her direction and in his or her presence. It should be signed with the testator's usual signature, whatever form that takes. You should bear in mind, though, that anything extreme, such as using a nickname, may mean that the court will in due time require evidence confirming that the will was signed properly.

The will should be signed immediately beneath the last line of the text (i.e., after the last line of words making the gift(s)). Although it is not necessarily invalid if it is signed elsewhere, there can be considerable delay when the will comes to be proved if evidence has to be obtained from the witnesses confirming that all was done properly.

Your signature should be legible and in such a form as to give rise to no doubts that you intended it to be in execution of your will. If you are unable to make a firm signature because of illness or accident, it is possible to make arrangements for someone else to sign the will on your behalf. If this is the case, it would probably be in your best interest to ask a solicitor to draw up your will, but if you do it yourself, please remember that the person signing the will on your behalf must do so in your presence at your request and in the presence of the witnesses. The attestation clause must state that the will was signed "on behalf of … and in his [or her] presence and at his [or her] direction …".

A "mark" (X) can be a signature to a will but here again it would be advisable to consult a solicitor before making your will if it is likely to be "signed" in this way. For the fee (which need not necessarily be large) you can have peace of mind.

There is no need for a stamp to be attached to a will before it is signed. For several years it was common to see a two-penny stamp at the bottom of the will with the signature of the testator written over it – this is quite unnecessary.

As has been mentioned before, the will should be signed "at the foot or end thereof" (that is, directly under the last line) if trouble is to be avoided. However, an amendment to the Wills Act 1837 means that a will may be proved if it has been signed by the testator anywhere, even on the back. Evidence of the intention of the testator when signing will be required by the court and if this can be provided, the will can be proved. There is a case on record where the testator signed the envelope in which the will was kept; the will was proved even though the document itself had not been signed. Signing in an unconventional place is not recommended, but this case again illustrates that the courts make every effort to accept a will.

Witnessing a Will

The other characteristic of a successful will is that it is witnessed properly. Again, this is a simple operation if the basic rules are followed.

It is a legal requirement in England and Wales for a will to be witnessed by two individuals, except in one instance which is discussed on page 22.

There is no age limit for witnesses, but they must be aware of what is happening and must be able to see the testator sign the will. This last requirement means that a blind person cannot act as a witness. Obviously, it is better to choose witnesses who are over eighteen and who are aware of the consequences of witnessing a will. It is not simply a matter of signing a piece of paper. There is a case on record in which the court held that the witnesses do not have to know they are signing a will; what they must be aware of is that they are witnessing someone's signature on an important document and must be aware of the identity of the testator and of the act they are performing. The act of witnessing a will involves certain obligations, not least of which is a duty to provide evidence to the court if, later, there is doubt or a dispute about the execution of the will. This is why it is important to ensure that the persons who witness your will are reliable and sensible.

An important point to remember is that any gift in the will to a witness of the will is void. Likewise, someone who is the husband, wife or civil partner of a witness at the time of witnessing would also lose any such gift. This provision of the Wills Act 1837 does not prevent a person named as an executor from being a competent witness. Nor does it apply to a beneficiary who subsequently marries or becomes the civil partner of one of the witnesses, but this is rather exceptional. To sum up, neither of your two witnesses should be a beneficiary under your will, or be married to, or the civil partner of, a beneficiary under your will.

Two individuals are required to act as witnesses. They must both be present when you sign your will and must both see you do it. There is one printed form of will which is accompanied by a photograph showing the correct method of signing and witnessing, but the instructions above should suffice. Remember, to be valid, the will must be signed by the testator in the presence of two witnesses, who must then sign in the presence of the testator. Although not strictly necessary, it is much better if all three meet for the signing, and sign one after each other – the testator first, followed by the witnesses. Although it is not a legal requirement it is preferable for the witnesses to add their addresses. Then, if a question arises and a witness has to be traced, the address at the time of signing is known.

Even if both witnesses do not see the testator sign, it may still be possible to prove the will. It is sufficient that both witnesses see the signature of the testator in his or her presence. This means that the will can be signed by the testator beforehand and produced by him or her for the witnesses to sign on a later occasion when he or she acknowledges his/her signature. This method is not recommended; it is mentioned only to demonstrate that a will which could be considered to be invalid may nevertheless be acceptable.

It is also possible for a will to be valid if the witnesses acknowledge their signatures in the presence of the testator, who has already signed the will (or acknowledged his or her signature) in their presence. Although this may seem confusing, it again serves to illustrate two points – that there is hope for almost any will, but that the more deviations from normal, the more complicated it is to put the will into effect.

There is one more point to take into account. Every will should contain confirmation that the procedures have been followed correctly. This takes the form of a statement made by the witnesses confirming that the will has been made properly. Technically, this is known as the "attestation clause" and every will should have one. In its simplest form, the words needed are "Signed by the testator/testatrix in our presence and then by us in his/hers." All printed will forms contain a clause such as this (it may be longer, but must still contain the essential elements), but if you are writing your own will on a blank piece of paper, you must include an attestation clause in the form set out above.

The testator should have signed the will immediately under the last line; the witnesses should sign to the side of, or directly beneath, the attestation clause (see the examples on pages 31 to 34).

Follow these simple guidelines and your will is a valid document. Do not forget to add the date it was signed. If you write the date on the back of the will as well as on the front (most printed will forms provide for this although it is not strictly necessary), make certain that both dates are the same. It is surprising how many wills contain two (and occasionally three) different dates. Although this is not necessarily fatal to the will's validity, it will cause delay when the time comes for it to be proved.

Summary of Formal Requirements

- A will must be in writing.
- A will must be signed by the person making it (the testator or testatrix) or by someone else at his/her direction and in his/her presence.
- The testator or testatrix must sign the will in the sight and presence of two witnesses.
- The witnesses must sign the will in the presence of the testator or testatrix after he/she has signed.
- It is important that the witnesses sign their names beneath the signature of the testator or testatrix. If this is not done, there may later be doubt about the way in which the will was signed, which could lead to complications when the will has to be proved.

- The will must be dated with the date upon which it was executed.
- Once your will has been executed, do not make any alterations to it. Do not change the address of yourself or of your executor or any beneficiaries if you or they move house (see page 23).
- If you wish to change anything in your will, either execute a codicil (see page 28) or make a completely new will.

Simultaneous Deaths of Husband and Wife

It is a sad fact of our times that husbands and wives may die together in road accidents or other disasters. Strictly, there is no such thing as "simultaneous death" in probate law – the term used is "died in circumstances rendering it uncertain who survived the other". A fine distinction perhaps, but one which illustrates that words and expressions do have precise meanings.

Some appointments of executors remain effective after the death of both spouses; for example "I appoint my husband and my son … to be my executors" enables the surviving executor, the son, to prove the will in the usual way even though the first executor, the husband, died with the testatrix. Difficulties arise if the only executor appointed by the will is the spouse who dies with the testator.

Under the law of England and Wales, where two people die and it is uncertain who survived the other, it is a general rule that the younger is assumed to have survived the elder. As general rules go, this is not too bad, but in the case of a husband or wife, it can cause an unequal distribution of the estate. Suppose a husband and wife make their wills, leaving everything to each other. There is nothing in either will saying what is to happen if they die together. The wife is younger than the husband and they have no children. They are both tragically killed in a road accident. In these circumstances, the husband's estate passes to the wife and then to her family. But the wife's estate, because she is considered to have survived her husband, passes directly to her next-of-kin, completely cutting out the husband's side of the family. This may be quite contrary to what they would have wished.

To avoid this, the wills could have provided for the possibility of dying together. In addition to the specific or residuary gift, the following words can be used, "If my husband and I die in circumstances rendering it uncertain who survived the other, I leave the remainder of my estate, both real and personal, to ...". Alternatively, the gift to the surviving spouse can be made to operate only on the survival being for a specified period, in which case the following words may be used: "Subject to ... surviving me by twenty-eight days I give ... but if ... shall fail to so survive me, I give ...".

Joint Wills

Although not particularly common in this country, the joint will is quite popular abroad. A joint will is two wills in one, not simply two individual wills written on the same piece of paper, but a complete integrated document commencing with the words "This is the last will and Testament of us ..." and throughout referring to all bequests and devises as made by "us".

Joint wills tend to be cumbersome (they have to be proved on the death of each testator) and offer no major advantages. Careful drafting is required if contradictions and pitfalls are to be avoided. A joint will should be drawn up by a solicitor.

Usually, a joint will is made by a husband and wife, each leaving all their estate to the other, with gifts to other parties on the death of the survivor. Even when this is the intention, a joint will is not recommended.

Privileged Wills

Earlier in the chapter (page 2), an exception to the general rule about how a will must be made was mentioned. This is the only exception that is allowed.

A will made while on actual military service by a soldier, sailor or airman, or by a seaman at sea, who is domiciled in England and Wales, does not have to comply with any of the formalities. It need not be witnessed, signed or even written down. The testator can be under eighteen years old and still the will can be proved.

This is of course extremely unusual and the rules allowing this type of will were designed for emergencies or other situations where the usual formalities cannot be complied with. The fact that the rules are relaxed only in unusual circumstances again demonstrates the strictness of the procedure for executing a will.

Alterations to a Will

A will should be a perfect document. No amendments, crossings-out, blots or other disfiguring marks should be present. Indeed, anything in a will which looks as though it might be an alteration is always investigated by the court. This does not mean that anything sinister happens, but it is quite possible that evidence will be required to establish at what stage during the making of the will the alteration was made.

Once you have made your will, do not attach (for example with a pin, paper clip or staple) any other document(s) to it. If you do, the court may take the view that there could have been other documents attached which formed part of the will and ought to be incorporated. Evidence may be required to deal with the pin, paper clip or staple marks.

There is a general presumption that any alterations to a will were made after the will was executed, and therefore they are not valid as they were not executed along with the rest of the will. If, though, a will was amended before execution, evidence of that, usually from one of the witnesses, would be accepted by the court so that the will can be proved as amended.

It is clearly preferable for the will to be written, typed or printed without errors. If you do make a mistake, amend it clearly and when you sign your will, initial the alteration and have the witnesses do the same. The presence of the initials of the testator and the witnesses should reduce the possibility of difficulties when the will is proved.

A better way to avoid trouble if you make a mistake is to tear up the incorrect document and start again. Remember, on no account should you make any alteration after you have executed your will unless you follow the procedure for re-executing it.

If you discover a mistake in your will, it is possible to amend it even after it has been executed, but the procedure is complicated. For the sake of completeness, it is set out below. The method of executing a will has already been described, and much the same method is used to re-execute it. There are two ways this can be done:

The amendment can be inserted at the appropriate place in the will, and a further attestation clause, referring to the amendment and including the date, added to the bottom. The following words can be used where the alteration consists of adding words:

"Signed by the testator
in re-execution of his last
Will and Testament on
... 20..., in the presence
of us and by us in his   (*Signature of testator*)
presence, the words "..."
having been added to the
Will.

(*Signature*)   (*Signature*)
  Ellen Fotheringale   George Harrow
  15 Acacia Road   11 Acacia Road
  Middlemarch   Middlemarch
  Loamshire MD6 9JS   Loamshire MD6 9JS"

Alternatively, the amendment can be made to the will and the testator and the witnesses sign in the margin next to the amendment. An attestation clause like that set out above should also be written in.

As you can see, the procedure for amending an executed will is complicated, which perhaps accounts for the fact that it is used infrequently.

Amending a will by executing an additional document – a codicil – is described later (see page 28).

Dissolution of Marriage or Civil Partnership

Divorce is perhaps the last subject in mind when making a will, but the United Kingdom has the highest divorce rate in Europe. Until 1982, a divorce did not have any effect on a will. Unless a further will or codicil was made, or the will was revoked (see below), the provisions of the will were completely unaffected by the divorce. If a wife died leaving a will giving everything to her husband, he would inherit it even if the couple had been divorced for years by the time she died. But the Administration of Justice Act 1982 changed this by stating that the terms of a will would be altered if there had been a divorce. Two parts to the will were affected: the appointment of executors and gifts to the ex-spouse.

This was again changed by the Law Reform (Succession) Act 1995 which amended the Wills Act 1837 and applies to all wills made by persons who were married and die on or after 1 January 1996. The 1837 Act was further amended by the Civil Partnership Act 2004. The effect of this amendment is to equate the wills of civil partners with those of married persons. So if a civil partnership is dissolved, the wills of those partners are treated in the same way as a husband or wife's will after their marriage is dissolved.

If you are making your will now, clearly the amended 1837 Act applies. It provides that in the event of the dissolution of a marriage or civil partnership, the appointment of the ex-spouse or partner as executor, and any gift to him or her, does not take effect. The ex-spouse or partner is treated as if he or she had died on the date of the decree absolute, in other words, as if he or she had pre-deceased the person making the will. In consequence, any provision in the will which was to take effect should the then-spouse or partner have died (for example, an alternative appointment of executor or gift of the estate) comes into force. This is particularly useful as otherwise the estate would have been undisposed of; it will save the alternative provisions (which the testator wanted to make) rather than substitute something which the testator may not have wanted.

The provisions of the Wills Act 1837, as amended, apply only in the absence of any words in the will indicating that the terms of the will are to take effect even if the testator's marriage or civil partnership has been dissolved.

It is possible to provide in your will for the prospect of dissolution, but words such as "If my marriage to ... has been dissolved at the date of my death ..." may not seem appropriate, especially as the will eventually becomes a public document. It is difficult to express a gift discreetly, but words such as "If my wife does not survive me, or if the gift to her lapses for any reason, then ..." might be appropriate. There have been few wills so far affected by this provision and it is difficult to advise with any degree of certainty, but the wording given above has been used and is now considered acceptable by the court.

Inheritance Act Claims

If a will makes insufficient or no provision for a spouse, former spouse, partner, children or certain others who were maintained by a deceased person while he or she was alive, those disinherited are entitled to apply to a court to have the provisions of the will varied in their favour. This is explained in more detail on pages 132 to 134. If you are making a will but do not wish to provide for those who are dependent on you, you should seek professional help with your will. This may avoid costly court proceedings after your death.

Revocation of a Will

So far, the emphasis has been on making a will, but there may come a time when you wish to change the provisions of your will. If you wish to make a simple amendment or a small adjustment, a codicil (see page 28) may be the answer. However, to make a major amendment, it may be better to revoke your will and make another. This means that the first will must in some way be disposed of so that the later will can take full effect. There are several ways in which this can be done.

Destruction

The easiest way to revoke your will is to tear it up or destroy it in some other way. You must do this yourself or someone else must do it for you at your direction and *in your presence*. Many wills are destroyed by third parties in the absence of the testator. This means the revocation is not effective, which can in turn cause much difficulty at a later date. Another hazard of revocation by destruction is that it leaves you without a will, and although you may intend to make another straight away, it is perhaps safer to use the next method to revoke your old will.

Another Will

Revocation of a will may be carried out by stating that you have done so in your new will. The inclusion of the words "I hereby revoke all former wills and codicils made by me and declare this to be my last will and testament" is sufficient. Instead of "wills and codicils" you may use the words "testamentary documents", which is simply another way of referring to both wills and codicils.

The "revocation" clause is an essential part of a will and should always be included. There is nothing to stop you destroying your old will once you have made your new one but before doing so make absolutely certain that your latest will has been executed properly, for an invalid will has no effect upon anything; it would not even be effective to revoke an earlier will.

Marriage or Civil Partnership

It has already been seen that dissolution of a testator's marriage or civil partnership does not revoke a will, although it affects its provisions. Marriage or the formation of a civil partnership, on the other hand, does affect a will made earlier. Ever since the Wills Act 1837, a will is revoked if the testator marries after making that will. A further section was inserted into the 1837 Act with effect from 5 December 2005 by the Civil Partnership Act 2004, providing that the will of a testator is revoked by his or her forming a civil partnership.

It is as well to remember that many people diagnosed with a terminal illness regulate their relationship with a partner by marrying or forming a civil partnership with some haste before events prevent it. Perhaps not surprisingly they forget that a will made to benefit the partner is revoked by that marriage or civil partnership.

This is the general rule, but it does not apply if the terms of the will make clear that the will is to remain in force if the testator marries or forms a civil partnership after executing it. This is known as a will "made in contemplation of marriage" or "in contemplation of forming a civil partnership". Although there is no standard wording for such a clause, the following is an example:

> "This Will is made in contemplation of my forthcoming marriage with … and should not be revoked thereby. [If my said marriage with … does not take place within … months of the date hereof, this Will shall be of no effect and if I should die unmarried within the period of … months, this Will shall be of no effect]."

The sentence in square brackets is optional, defining further the terms under which the will is to remain effective. If there is no clause or other indication that a will is to remain effective if the testator marries or forms a civil partnership, the will is revoked by the marriage or the formation of the partnership.

It is fairly straightforward to revoke a will, but suppose you do not wish to revoke your will in its entirety, but simply add a number of gifts, or amend some of the terms? You need not go to all the trouble of making another will. A codicil will do.

Codicils

A codicil is a document which modifies the terms of a will. It is made in exactly the same manner as a will and all the formalities which govern the making, signing and witnessing of a will apply equally to a codicil. In effect, the codicil is a mini-will and has the effect of changing the date of the will to the date of the codicil. The codicil is part of the will and is proved at the same time. It can have the effect of making valid an invalid will if the codicil is properly executed and confirms the will. The "confirming of the will" is simply a clause, usually inserted at the end of the codicil, which states that the will remains as it was, subject to the amendments made in the codicil. For an example of this and of other parts of the codicil, see page 29.

A codicil can revoke a will, and if the testator makes no other will, he or she dies intestate. This is rare but it has happened. More constructive ways of making codicils are discussed next.

The codicil should refer to the will by date, and should set out clearly the part or parts of the will to be modified, and the modification. This must be expressed in the clearest possible terms. For example, if both the codicil and the will contain gifts to the same person, the codicil should make clear whether the second gift is as well as, or instead of, the earlier one. Disputes often arise on this point, simply because the codicil was not clearly expressed. Any part of the will can be modified by a codicil and any number of codicils can be made. It is not unknown for seven or eight codicils to be proved along with the will, but this is rare and if there are as many amendments as this, it is probably wise to make a new will. Apart from the inherent dangers in so many amending documents, the making of a new will, incorporating all the amendments, simplifies the administration of the estate.

If subsequent codicils are made, they should be numbered (first, second, third and so on) and each referred to in the subsequent codicils, by both date and number. It is important to recite the date of the will and previous codicils correctly, as any mistakes must be investigated by the court when the time comes to prove the documents.

A codicil can be revoked in the same way as a will, but there are one or two points which are worth bearing in mind.

If a codicil revokes part of your will and the codicil is itself later revoked, the will remains as it was immediately after the first revoking codicil was made. It is not possible to restore your will simply by revoking the document which carried out the revocation. If you want to do this, you must either make a codicil restoring the revoked part of your will specifically, or make a new will. The latter is advisable.

A revoked codicil must be proved (unless it has been revoked by destruction) and should on no account be destroyed or thrown away. Each application to the probate registry is carefully examined and one of the numerous checks concerns the numbering of the codicils. If any are missing, questions will be asked.

Although there is probably no such thing as a typical codicil, the following illustrates all the points which have been mentioned:

> This is the first codicil of me, Frederick Joseph Bloggs, to my last Will and Testament dated 10th July 1998. In paragraph 2 of my said Will I made a gift of £100 to John Arthur Smith of 17 Acacia Gardens, Middlemarch, Loamshire MD5 6TG. I revoke that gift and in substitution I give the sum of £500 to the said John Arthur Smith.
>
> I leave the sum of £50 to Jeremy Cole of Holly House, Ivy Road, Middlemarch, Loamshire MD3 5GF.
>
> In all other respects I confirm my said Will.

Dated 5 January 2008

Signed by the above-named	
Frederick Joseph Bloggs the	*Signature of testator)*
testator in the presence of	
us and by us in his presence	
(Signature)	*(Signature)*
Ellen Fotheringale	George Harrow
15 Acacia Road	11 Acacia Road
Middlemarch	Middlemarch
Loamshire MD1 3DF	Loamshire MD1 3DF

Safe-keeping

Having made your will, it should be kept in a safe place and your executors should know where it is. Most people who make a will without going to a solicitor keep it themselves. This is simple, but do make certain your executors know where to find it. Alternatively, a bank will look after your will, usually for a fee.

If you have a solicitor to draw up your will, the firm will probably keep the original and give you a copy.

Even if you make your will yourself, you can still have it kept in safe custody until it is required. For a single payment the court will keep your will, record that they have it, and produce it to your executors when the time comes to prove it. You may lodge your will at the Principal Registry of the Family Division in London, or at any district probate registry or sub-registry (see page 151 for the addresses), although all such wills are sent to the Principal Registry for storage. You may either go in person to lodge it, or (to the Principal Registry only) send it by post. If anyone else does this on your behalf, the registry will require confirmation in writing that you have given your authority. The correct procedure will be explained to you when you apply. It involves signing the official envelope in which the will is kept and you will receive a receipt from the court. The fee for all this is £15.

You may withdraw your will from deposit at any time, but you will have to write to the Principal Registry requesting its return. There is no fee for this.

When the time comes for the will to be proved, it must be withdrawn from safe keeping. Proof of death (a death certificate) will be necessary, and it is quite likely that the executors will need to have a copy of the will made and file it with the court before the original is released. For a small fee, the registry will make the necessary copy. A receipt from the persons to whom the will is sent will also be required.

This is not a complicated procedure, and if you are in any doubt that your will might not be found after your death, or fear that you may mislay it, "safe custody" is the answer. Secrecy is assured; the will is securely stored and the service is inexpensive.

Examples

Set out below are four sample wills. They illustrate complete wills, but readers are reminded that they are examples only; you should not follow one of these wills when making your own unless you are quite certain that it is appropriate for your circumstances. Wills (c) and (d) in particular are complex and it has been noted that in cases like this professional help should be sought.

Will Leaving Everything to Spouse

I, Andrew Brown, of 13 Acacia Road, Middlemarch, Loamshire MD1 2JX hereby declare this to be my last Will. I revoke all former wills and codicils made by me. I appoint my wife Clarissa Brown to be my sole executrix and devise and bequeath the whole of my estate, both real and personal, to her absolutely.

Dated 21st January 2008.
Signed by the said Andrew
Brown the testator in our   (*Signature of testator*)
presence and by us in his

(*Signature*)	(*Signature*)
Ellen Fotheringale	George Harrow
15 Acacia Road	11 Acacia Road
Middlemarch	Middlemarch
Loamshire MD1 3JX	Loamshire MD1 3JX

Will Leaving Bulk of Estate to One Person with Other Gifts, including Another Gift if the Main Beneficiary does not Survive

I, Andrew Brown, of 13 Acacia Road, Middlemarch, Loamshire MD4 3LX hereby declare this to be my last Will. I revoke all former wills and codicils made by me. I appoint Laurence Kelly of 2 Shakespeare Drive, Arden, Globeshire AR8 9FX and John Falstaff of 5 Verona Walk, Middlesbury MI8 4HY to be my executors. I leave the sum of £2000 to each of the following persons:

(i)   Charles Davies of 15 Figtree Walk, Eastwick, Loamshire EA4 5GH;

(ii)   Eleanor Smith of 6 Peachtree Street, Lowville, Barsetshire LO4 5HG;

(iii) Isabel Brown of 17 Appledown Way, Highville, Wessex FS3 4TY.

I leave the remainder of my estate, both real and personal, to the said John Falstaff.

Dated 21st January 2008
Signed by the said Andrew
Brown the testator in our   (*Signature of testator*)
presence and by us in his

(*Signature*)   (*Signature*)
Ellen Fotheringale   George Harrow
15 Acacia Road   11 Acacia Road
Middlemarch   Middlemarch
Loamshire MD1 2JX   Loamshire MD1 2JX

More Complex Will made by a Blind Testator
I, Annette Mary White, of 79 Acacia Road, Middlemarch, Loamshire MD5 8PL hereby declare this to be my last Will. I revoke all former wills and codicils made by me.

I appoint Mary Kelly of 2 Shakespeare Drive, Arden, Globeshire AR8 9FX and Helen Falstaff of 5 Verona Walk, Middlesbury, Loamshire MD4 2JX to be executrixes but should either of them not survive me by thirty days or renounce probate or be incapable of acting as my executrix I appoint Georgina Newton of 7 Pond Street, Middlemarch, Loamshire MD11 2JX to take the place of either of my executrixes so unable to prove my will or of both if both are so unable.

I leave the following pecuniary bequests:
(i)   £100 to Charlotte Davies of 15 Figtree Walk, Sometown, Anyshire SM6 7DY;
(ii) £250 to Eleanor Smith of 16 Peachtree Street, Lowville, Barsetshire BX8 9PY with the proviso that should she not survive me the said sum should go to her husband Andrew John Smith;
(iii) £100 to the Society for the Preservation of Ancient Civil Servants of 7A Grand Buildings, Crumbletown, Doddershire DO9 7FS and hereby declare that the receipt of the Treasurer of the said Society shall be sufficient discharge for my executors;
(iv) £50 each to Trevor Underhill and Susan Underhill both of Hill House, Slope Avenue, Uptown,

Loamshire UP5 6HY. Such sum to be held in trust for them until they respectively attain the age of eighteen years by their parents Alan John Underhill and Barbara Joan Underhill jointly.

I leave the remainder of my estate, both real and personal to the following persons:

    (i)   50 per cent to the said Charlotte Davies with the proviso that should she not survive me by thirty days, this gift shall be paid to her husband, Frederick Archibald Davies;

    (ii)   25 per cent to Roberta Frances Appleyard of 99 Fruit Cage Walk, London E39 5TY;

    (iii)   25 per cent to Paulina Rose Quayle and her husband George Alan Quayle jointly both of 17 Optimists Row, Hopetown, Loamshire HO9 8TR with the proviso that should either the said Paulina Rose Quayle or George Alan Quayle die in my lifetime, the whole of the said gift shall be paid to the survivor.

Dated 21st July 2008.

Signed by the said Annette Mary White
the testatrix (by her mark) the Will
having first been read over to the said
Annette Mary White by Mary Rose
Shipp of 101 Acacia Road,
Middlemarch, Loamshire MD1 2JX in
our presence when the said Annette
Mary White seemed perfectly to
understand the same and approve the
contents thereof in our presence and by
us in hers.

(*Signature*)	(*Signature*)
Ellen Fotheringale	George Harrow
15 Acacia Road	11 Acacia Road
Middlemarch	Middlemarch
Loamshire MD1 2JX	Loamshire MD1 2JX

A Will Leaving the Estate to Two Children and Appointing Guardians, there being No one with Parental Responsibility for the Children

I, Andrew Brown, of 13 Acacia Road, Middlemarch, Loamshire MD1 5PX hereby declare this to be my last Will. I revoke all former testamentary dispositions made by me. I appoint Charles Davies and Eleanor Davies both of 15 Figtree Walk, Sometown, Loamshire SO9 9NB to be my executors and the guardians of my children Georgina Brown and Harriet Brown should either or both be under the age of eighteen years at the date of my death.

I leave all my estate, both real and personal, to the said Charles Davies and Eleanor Davies upon trust for the said Georgina Brown and Harriet Brown in equal shares absolutely. Should either or both of the said Georgina Brown and Harriet Brown be under the age of eighteen years at the date of my death the share is to be held by the said Charles Davies and Eleanor Davies upon trust and applied for the use and benefit of the minor child or children at their discretion. Upon the minor child or children attaining the age of eighteen years, the sum held on trust (both capital and interest) is to be paid to the child forthwith.

Dated 21st January 2008
Signed by the said Andrew
Brown the testator in our   (*Signature of testator*)
presence and by us in his
(*Signature*)   (*Signature*)
Ellen Fotheringale   George Harrow
15 Acacia Road   11 Acacia Road
Middlemarch   Middlemarch
Loamshire MD1 2JX   Loamshire MD1 2JX

Last Words on Wills

Three points should be mentioned before concluding this chapter.

If inheritance tax is payable (see Chapter 4), the gifts in the will (both money and personal effects) each attract a proportion of the tax payable. If you wish the specific gifts to be paid in full, so the recipient does not have to pay the tax, the addition of the words "free of tax" after the amount or gift will have the desired effect. It does not mean that the tax will not be payable at all. Instead, the residuary estate bears the tax due on the specific gift.

It is not the object of this book to give detailed advice on inheritance tax. If you wish to word your will in such a way as to minimise inheritance tax (which can be complicated), it is strongly suggested that you seek legal advice. It is not just a matter of wording; it may involve creating trusts.

Secondly, we have said nothing about the testator being "of sound mind". This is totally unnecessary and belongs firmly to murder-mystery plays set in the 1930s; so too does the ceremony of "reading the will", something which very rarely happens except on the stage.

Lastly, in none of the examples has there been any expression of personal feelings or farewell messages. The will, once proved, becomes a public document, open to anyone to read or copy, and is not the place to express intimate feelings. Similarly it is not the appropriate place to set out reasons for making a particular provision, or for not making a particular provision. A letter left with the will is a better way to do this.

The whole of this chapter has been devoted to making a will. What happens when you need to prove a will, and what to do if there is no will at all, are discussed in following chapters.

Chapter 2

Who May Apply

In this chapter we move on to explain what needs to be done following a death. This involves applying to the probate court for a "grant of representation" ("a grant"), locating all the property of the deceased person, paying the debts and ensuring that what is left goes to those who should have it. The task of doing all this belongs to the deceased's "personal representatives".

The expression "personal representatives" is a general term meaning "executors appointed by a will" and "administrators". In Chapter 1, how executors are appointed, and the reasons for doing so, were discussed. In this chapter the role of administrators and how they come into the picture will become clear.

The idea of applying to the probate court may seem daunting. Although the probate registries, as they are called, are indeed courts of law, you will not experience anything like the court scenes which feature in films and or on television. Instead, when the time comes, you will see a specially trained member of the court staff in a private room. This is explained in more detail in Chapter 6.

Why is a Grant of Representation Necessary?

Where the deceased has left a will, the executors need to obtain a grant of representation to give them authority to collect in and distribute the estate. The grant also confirms the validity of the will and therefore the executors' authority to distribute the estate in accordance with the terms of the will. If there is no will, a grant of representation gives the personal representatives the authority they need to deal with the deceased's property and affairs.

The personal representatives may of course, instruct a solicitor to apply for the grant and deal with the property. Indeed, this is recommended if you are in doubt about any aspect of the application, or if you think you may not be able to cope with sorting out the property. In addition to solicitors, certain other professionals – barristers and notaries – are also able to do this kind of work. On the other hand, you may wish to do it yourself. Although this is a difficult time for the bereaved, many find they can deal with a straightforward case on their own and, as they soon discover, the officers of the probate registries are sympathetic and helpful.

For simplicity, this chapter is written as if there is only one applicant for the grant. Obviously, if two people apply they act together and everything we say applies to both of them.

The Grant of Representation

The phrase "grant of representation" is a term as old as probate itself. The grant is the document supplied by the court which confirms the authenticity of the will if there is one; if there is no will, the grant enables the person named in it to take charge of the deceased's assets, pay the debts and distribute the rest to the persons entitled to it.

The term "grant" brings to mind an award of money and does sometimes cause misunderstandings. The court will not be involved in any way with finding or gathering together the money or other property of the deceased, or with passing it on to those who inherit it. These are the duties of the personal representatives. The function of the court is to supply the document which enables the personal representatives to carry out these duties.

"Grant of representation" is a general term that covers three types of grant – a "grant of probate", a "grant of letters of administration (with will)" and a "grant of letters of administration". The differences between the three will become apparent later in this chapter.

Illustrations of grants of representation are set out on pages 119–121.

Personal Application Department

If you have decided to apply for a grant yourself, you must first know where to apply. The Probate, Divorce and Admiralty Division of the High Court was established 150 years ago. At the same time the facility to apply for a grant of representation in person was confirmed, and it was provided that every registry (the registries are the "branch offices" of the Division) would have a special section to deal exclusively with personal applicants. Times change, but the Family Division, as this Division of the High Court is now called, still maintains the tradition and every registry and sub-registry accepts personal applications. The addresses of all these registries and sub-registries, together with the locations of the probate offices run by each, are set out on pages 151–153.

Probate offices are open only on certain days of the week (sometimes as infrequently as once every six weeks), and only then to applicants who have arranged appointments there, so you must address initial inquiries to a main registry or sub-registry, since these are open during normal office hours. In due time you will have to attend by appointment to be interviewed and complete the paperwork – this can be at the office nearest to you if you wish.

Obtaining the Application Forms

All the information you need (including the addresses of the various registries and sub-registries) is found in the application pack. This can be obtained in a number of ways; increasingly, applicants are downloading the forms from the Probate Service website (www.theprobateservice.gov.uk). This has the advantage that the documents are available immediately and the relevant information is readily to hand whenever you wish. There is also a link to the website of HM Revenue and Customs ("HMRC") where you can get information about inheritance tax and the relevant HMRC forms (inheritance tax is dealt with in Chapter 4). Alternatively you can apply for the forms to the Probate and Inheritance Tax Helpline (0845 302 0900), or telephone or call into your local probate registry or sub-registry.

Entitlement to the Grant

A grant issues only to the person or persons entitled to it. Who is entitled to apply depends upon whether or not the deceased person left a will. In the next two sections, we identify the people who may apply. We mentioned in the introduction to this chapter that they are known as the "personal representative(s)" of the deceased person and are either executor(s) appointed by a will, or administrator(s). It should be remembered that a maximum of four persons are entitled to apply for a grant.

Who May Apply for a Grant Where There is a Will

In order of priority, those entitled to apply for a grant if the deceased left a will are:

Executors

Executors have the first right to prove a will and take the grant of representation, whether or not any legacy has been left to them. An executor is appointed by the testator and is the person entitled to have the will when the testator dies. Clearly, the executor is the best person to apply for the grant and that is what usually happens.

Where there is more than one executor, each has an equal right to prove the will, but if they do not all apply, the executor(s) applying must tell the others about the application. Of course, it is much better to act together and most executors do so.

If an executor does not wish to apply for the grant of representation, he or she is free to "renounce" probate; this is explained in more detail on page 42.

Residuary Beneficiaries

The executors appointed in the will may not, when the time comes, be able to apply for probate – they may themselves have died or may, perhaps because of illness, decline to do so. They may simply not wish to be involved. If they do decline to act, they must "renounce probate", giving up their rights completely to someone else (see page 42). In such a case, the persons entitled to apply for a grant are the residuary beneficiaries. As explained on pages 12–15, the residuary beneficiary or beneficiaries are those who inherit what remains in the estate after any specific gifts.

There is an order in which residuary beneficiaries may apply for probate. A "residuary legatee or devisee in trust" has the right to apply in preference to any other type of residuary beneficiary. If the gift of residue is given "upon trust to Andrew Brown", the gift going on to state those persons to whom Andrew Brown is eventually to give the money, then Andrew Brown is "a residuary legatee and devisee in trust".

If there is no residuary legatee and devisee in trust, the residuary beneficiary for life (that is, one who inherits property only for his or her lifetime) or an ordinary residuary beneficiary, is entitled to apply. If there is more than one, they are equally entitled. All other types of residuary beneficiary have an equal right to apply after the residuary legatee and devisee in trust.

If you think you may be able to apply as residuary legatee or devisee but are unsure, it is a good plan to inquire at the probate registry. Even if it turns out that you are not entitled, the registry will clarify the correct way to proceed.

People Entitled to Undisposed of Estate

We have already seen (page 15) that undisposed of estate is the property not disposed of by the will. We have also noted that there is no residuary beneficiary if the will failed to name one, or if the residuary beneficiary died before the testator and there was no "saving clause". If there are no executors who can apply for the grant, and if there is no residuary beneficiary under the will, the laws of intestacy are used to identify who can apply for the grant and the matter is dealt with as if there were no will. In this situation, the intestacy rules determine not only who is to receive the undisposed of property, but also who is entitled to apply for the grant. The list, in order of entitlement to apply for grant, is given on pages 43–44.

Although it is unusual, it is possible to have residuary beneficiaries and undisposed of estate under the same will. In these circumstances all the beneficiaries have equal title to apply for the grant and prove the will.

Specific Beneficiaries

In the absence of any of the people mentioned in the order set out above, people to whom specific gifts are left are entitled to apply to prove the will. It is quite a common error to suppose that in these circumstances the person who is left the largest sum in the will is entitled to apply in preference to the others. This is not the case, and any specific legatee or devisee is entitled to apply. For example, in the case of a will which, although not making any residuary gift, nevertheless disposes of the whole of the estate by setting out every item specifically, any of the beneficiaries is entitled to apply for a grant.

Surprising as it may seem, creditors of the deceased, who may not even be related, are entitled equally with specific beneficiaries to apply for a grant. Although it is unusual for a creditor to make a personal application, if the deceased person owed you money, and no one else seems prepared to take on the administration of the estate, it may be worth considering it. Indeed, this may be the only way to obtain payment of the debt, but you would have to undertake the administration of the whole estate, not just the part owed to you.

Set out below is the list of people who usually apply to prove a will, in order of their entitlement to do so. Put more formally, applications to prove a will are made by those persons entitled to apply under Rule 20 of the Non-Contentious Probate Rules 1987, who are as follows:

(1) the executor(s);

(2) any residuary legatee or devisee holding the estate in trust for any other person;

(3) any other residuary legatee or devisee or any person entitled to the undisposed of residue of the estate. This is subject to the points set out in (iv) above, which describe what happens when the estate has been disposed of totally, even if there is no gift of residue. In the absence of any relations entitled to the undisposed of estate, the Crown may make the claim;

(4) the personal representative of any residuary legatee or devisee (except a residuary legatee or devisee holding the estate in trust or for life) (in other words, the administrator of the estate of a residuary beneficiary, except one holding the residuary estate in trust, who died after the person whose will is now being proved);

(5) any legatee or devisee or creditor;

(6) the personal representative of any legatee or devisee (except a legatee or devisee holding the estate in trust or for life) or creditor (see explanation in (4) above).

You may notice that the fourth and sixth groups above were not mentioned earlier in this discussion. A "personal representative" in this context is someone who has obtained a grant of representation to the estate of a residuary or specific legatee or devisee, or a creditor, where that legatee, devisee or creditor has himself or herself died after the person whose will we are now discussing. This is a rare situation, but the rule is necessary to establish the entitlement to a grant in the estate of someone who died some time ago, but either the will was not proved, or it was proved by someone who has since died without finishing the administration of the estate. This is complex, but it is included for the sake of completeness. It also shows that it is nearly always possible to find someone who can make the application for the grant.

The personal application staff at the registry will always help work out who may apply for the grant. They need to have all the facts, although it may not always be possible to answer your question at once. Complex points may require consideration before an answer can be given. If your case is complicated, you may need to write, or even call in, to the registry when you make your application for the grant.

Renouncing Probate

If an executor does not wish to administer the estate, he or she is not obliged to do so, and may instead "renounce", by completing a form which the probate registry supplies. If you are one of several executors and do not wish to act at present but do not wish to give up your right altogether, you may reserve the right to apply later. This must be set out in the form of application for probate (see page 77). The registry will then send to the applicant a small form for signing by the executor who does not wish to act for the time being. In a case like this, the grant, when issued, will show that power to apply for a grant has been "reserved" to the executor in question.

Who May Apply for a Grant Where There is No Will

If someone dies without having made a will, the persons who may apply for a grant of representation are the persons who are entitled to inherit the deceased's property. The question of who inherits the deceased's property and who is entitled to apply to the court for a grant are one and the same.

Chapter 1 dealt at length with the advantages of making a will and "the law of intestacy" was mentioned. It was noted that people who leave a will are said to die "testate". Those who die without making a will are described as having died "intestate".

The laws governing what happens to the property of someone who dies intestate are based on a survey of the provisions of wills proved over a period of years. The order of persons entitled to share the property of someone who dies intestate was formulated to reflect what was most commonly done by those who did write wills. The list has undergone a number of changes since it was first formulated, the most recent being the inclusion of "civil partners". Briefly, a civil partner is someone who has undergone a civil partnership ceremony with someone of the same sex, and as a result the partners have the same legal footing as a married couple.

The order is as follows:

(1) the surviving spouse or civil partner (but there is a limit on how much the spouse or civil partner can inherit – see below);

(2) children or issue of children who died in the lifetime of the intestate (we have already seen that "issue" means children, grandchildren, great grandchildren and so on);

(3) parents;

(4) brothers or sisters, or the issue of brothers or sisters (nephews and nieces) who died in the lifetime of the intestate. Brothers or sisters here means brothers or sisters "of the whole blood" – that is, brothers and sisters who have the same mother and father;

(5) half brothers or sisters, or the issue of half brothers or sisters who died in the lifetime of the intestate. Half brothers and sisters has its ordinary meaning – brothers or sisters who have the same mother or father but not both;

(6) grandparents;

(7) uncles or aunts of the whole blood, or the issue of such uncles or aunts (cousins) who died in the lifetime of the intestate;

(8) half uncles or aunts, or the issue of half uncles or aunts who died in the lifetime of the intestate;

(9) the Crown;

(10) creditors.

See also pages 139–145.

With the exception of the surviving spouse or civil partner in (1) above, to qualify to have entitlement, the relationship as listed above need not be lawful. In other words, an illegitimate child, for example, is entitled to share in an estate equally with a legitimate child.

Groups (2) to (10) above are mutually exclusive. This means that, starting at the top of the list, if one person in a particular section in a class is alive, that person takes priority over all those in the classes below. The best way to explain this further is to give an example:

> The intestate is a widower who has died without children and both his parents are dead. He has two surviving sisters of the whole blood and a surviving half brother. A look at the list shows that the whole of the deceased's property will be shared between his two sisters to the exclusion of anyone else.

The surviving spouse or civil partner of someone who does not leave a will is entitled only to the goods and chattels and to a certain sum of money. The amount is determined by the date of death. The current figure, which applies where death occurred on or after December 1993, is £125,000 when the intestate left issue; and £200,000 when the intestate left no issue but was survived by parents, or brothers or sisters of the whole blood, or the issue of brothers or sisters of the whole blood who died in the lifetime of the intestate (see pags 140–142). The fixed sum of money which the surviving spouse or civil partner inherits is often called "the statutory legacy" because it is provided for by Act of Parliament. If the intestate died without being survived by any of these persons (issue, parents, brothers or sisters of the whole blood or their issue) then, and only then, the surviving spouse or civil partner is entitled to the whole of the estate.

It is clear from this that the popular concept that the surviving spouse or civil partner inherits the whole of the estate is not correct. The survivor does not even receive the major part of the estate over the fixed sums mentioned. If the deceased left children, the surviving spouse or civil partner has a life interest in one half of the excess over the fixed sum (the term "life interest" is explained below) and if the deceased left no children, but parents, or brothers or sisters or their issue, the surviving spouse or civil partner is entitled to one half of the estate over the fixed sum outright. As you can see, both these restrictions have the effect of cutting down the survivor's share in the estate, in some cases quite considerably. It can even result in the matrimonial home having to be sold in order to satisfy the claims of people whom it is quite possible the deceased may never have met.

Turning to the meaning of a "life interest", we noted in Chapter 1 that such an interest can be created by a will, and it has been mentioned above that a life interest may also arise when someone dies without leaving a will. Although a life interest arising under an intestacy does differ from one created by a will, there are similarities between the two. Both convey a limited gift and both describe how long that gift is to be enjoyed – the recipient is to have the property in question for his or her lifetime only, and the person making the gift stipulates who is to have it when the person with the life interest dies.

Life interests under a will and under an intestacy differ in two aspects, however. The first is that there is no voluntary element with a life interest under an intestacy. The terms are laid down by statute and there is no variation. The second difference, and the one which is important when working out who may apply for a grant, is that where there is a life interest under an intestacy (and this includes those life interests arising from undisposed of estate), two persons must apply for the grant, unless a district judge of the Principal Registry or a registrar of a district probate registry directs otherwise. As he or she will make such a direction only in exceptional circumstances, it is a good general rule to state that two applicants are required. The surviving spouse will clearly be one of the applicants, and the second applicant will be one of the people entitled next in order of priority to the estate. If there is no obvious second applicant, it is best not to delay making your application but to submit your papers to the registry of your choice. The matter can be sorted out at that stage.

Where there is no surviving spouse or civil partner and several persons are entitled to benefit, then any of them may apply alone, or any two or more of them (subject to a maximum of four) may apply jointly. If there is a dispute about who is to apply, application must be made to a district judge or registrar to determine who are to be the administrator(s).

If you are not certain you are entitled to apply for a grant, it is always worth an inquiry at your local registry or sub-registry. Although you may feel tempted to telephone, it is better to write or e-mail setting out the facts, or call in and have a talk with a member of staff. In certain circumstances it is even possible for you to act on behalf of someone who is entitled to apply for a grant, by becoming that person's attorney under a power of attorney.

It is worth mentioning that little harm is likely to result if an application is made by someone who does not fall clearly into any of the categories of people entitled to apply. Many applications are made by people who have no apparent right and yet eventually obtain the grant. So, if it turns out that you cannot make the application yourself, you may well be able to contact someone who can, after discussing the case with an officer of the registry.

A final word about the list on pages 43–44. You will notice that number (9) on the list is the Crown. In the absence of any of the persons listed in (1) to (8), the Crown is entitled to the estate.

Missing Family Members

Personal applicants often enquire about missing persons who may be entitled to the estate. It may be that the deceased person married and subsequently separated, and the spouse has not been seen for years. Suppose the deceased person did not make a will and was never divorced or judicially separated, so that the living spouse is entitled to most, if not all, of the estate. Who then is entitled to apply? There is no universal answer to questions of this kind; so much depends on the details of the case, but most problems do have a solution (not always to the liking of the applicant) and the only way to find out is to ask.

In a case like this, where it is difficult to work out who is entitled to the deceased person's property, the best advice the probate registries can give is to seek the help of a solicitor – not necessarily to take out the grant (which would not be so much of a problem) but to administer the estate. Bear in mind, first, that the role of the probate registries is to issue grants of representation only – they can play no part in, and cannot advise on, the question of who is to inherit the deceased's property; and second, that the issue of a grant does not itself give any right to the applicant to benefit from the estate.

Power of Attorney

In the discussion above it has been assumed that the person first entitled to the grant will actually make the application. This is indeed what usually happens, but in some circumstances it is impracticable. There are many reasons why a person entitled may not wish to take a grant, for example physical incapacity, a prolonged stay abroad, work commitments or simply not wanting to. It is not within the scope of this book to detail all the various types of application which can be made in those situations, but there is one which is becoming increasingly common and deserves to be mentioned.

There is a document which is in wide use in many areas of the law called a "power of attorney". This is an authority given by one person (the donor) to another (the donee or attorney) to act on the donor's behalf, either in all matters, or in some particular matter. The power of attorney enables the person named in it (the attorney) to act on behalf of the person who signs it (the donor). This means that the appointed executor, or other person entitled to apply for a grant, can appoint someone else to take the grant and administer the estate on his or her behalf.

Where such a power of attorney already exists and confers the appropriate power, the attorney may apply for a grant on behalf of the donor, where that person is entitled to apply under a will or intestacy. Alternatively, a power of attorney may be executed specifically to enable someone to act on behalf of the person entitled to apply for a grant.

There is also a special type of power of attorney called an enduring or lasting power of attorney which continues in force even if the donor becomes mentally incapable, provided of course that he or she was capable when the power of attorney was executed.

This is a special type of document which would not be supplied by the probate registry as it is more frequently used in connection with other matters, and would generally have been executed some time before the need to apply for a grant arises. If, though, an enduring or lasting power of attorney is in force, it is sufficient to enable the attorney to apply for a grant on behalf of the donor.

The lasting power of attorney replaced the enduring power of attorney and, since 1 October 2007, it has no longer been possible to make an enduring power of attorney, although one made prior to that date continues in force. The lasting power of attorney is very similar in scope, but there are two types of lasting power and it is the one dealing with financial matters (called a "property and affairs lasting power of attorney") which can be used only in these circumstances. Further information about enduring and lasting powers of attorney and their functions is available at the website of the Public Guardianship Office (www.guardianship.gov.uk).

If you have agreed to apply for a grant on behalf of someone else who is entitled to do so and no power of attorney is already in force, the probate registry will supply the necessary form by which you can be given authority. This is a straightforward power of attorney; the registries do not supply forms for making a lasting power of attorney. You will then have to take or send it to the person who is entitled to apply for the grant (the "donor" of the power of attorney). The power of attorney should be signed by the donor in the presence of a disinterested witness – a person who is not connected with the estate or the application, such as a next-door neighbour. The witness should sign his or her name and add the address.

Small Estates

One last point before moving on to the procedure for applying for a grant is that there are some situations where you need not make an application at all.

The purpose of the grant of representation is to enable the executor or administrator to receive and pass on the deceased's property. It provides organisations which hold property (banks and building societies, for example) with authority to release money to the person to whom the grant has been issued. Normally, of course, they could not pay out to anyone except the account holder. Where a grant has been issued, the asset holders can pay out the money in complete confidence that the court has decided that the person named in the grant is the correct one to administer the estate.

However, sometimes it is not necessary to obtain a grant at all in order to obtain the money. The Administration of Estates (Small Payments) Act 1965 enables organisations such as building societies and friendly societies to pay out sums of money to the person entitled to receive them up to an amount of £5,000. It is stressed that the Act *allows* these organisations to make payments; it does not *compel* them to do so. Consequently, you should not necessarily expect to receive payment just because the sum of money is below £5,000. Any bank or building society must safeguard its account holders (living or not), so it may lay down terms and conditions before releasing the assets. Quite what form these take depends on the organisation concerned, but if you have to collect assets from several holders you may be better advised to obtain a grant because then you will have only one set of formalities to go through, rather than a different set for each asset holder. Often the bank or building society requires you to sign an indemnity to cover the bank or building society if something goes wrong. Indemnities are discussed at page 61.

Chapter 3

The Estate

Identifying the Assets and Liabilities

One of the first tasks is to ascertain exactly what the deceased person left – not just all the property, but also the debts. "Property" includes not just a house or land, but stocks and shares, money in bank accounts or building societies, National Savings, Premium Bonds and pensions from employers or lump sums from insurance companies.

There are two main reasons for tracing the property and debts. In the first place, it is an obvious preliminary to ensuring that the property is distributed in accordance with the will, or, if there is no will, in accordance with the intestacy rules. Secondly, it provides the basis for valuing the estate, which in turn will determine whether or not inheritance tax (see Chapter 4) must be paid. Whether or not the probate registry will charge a fee also depends on the net value of the estate, the net value being the total value of all assets less any debts. "Values" are the values of each asset at the date of death. If the net value is below £5,000, no fee is payable. Estates above £5,000 attract a fee of £90. Fees are dealt with on page 111. Clearly, therefore, all the deceased's property and debts must be traced and quantified values ascertained before an application for a grant can be made. The task falls to the person or persons who wish to administer the estate – the personal representatives, who, as we have already seen, may be the executor(s) appointed by the will or the administrators.

As before, for ease of reference, this chapter is written as though there is only one person dealing with the estate. Obviously, if there are two (or more) executors or administrators, their duties are joint duties.

Most people keep details of their financial affairs, and their important papers, such as deeds, share certificates and building society passbooks, in a safe place either at home or at the bank. Often such papers are kept with the will. The person dealing with the estate should search carefully and make enquiries at the appropriate bank(s) and other organisations to make sure everything is found. Each bank or building society should be asked for a balance, including accrued interest, up to the date of death. Similarly, letters should be written seeking details of amounts due from pensions or annuities, including state pensions and benefits, and other sources of the deceased's income. Any cash found at the deceased's home should be removed and held securely until the executor or administrator is in a position to open an estate account with a bank or building society (see page 60).

Many people now manage their bank or building society accounts on-line. These accounts require the account holder to enter, at least, an identification code and password to gain entry to the account. This may cause a problem if, as is to be expected, there is no written record of the deceased's identification and password. But there is usually something to indicate that the deceased held such an account, and enquiry must be made of the account holder to ascertain the balance and any interest due to the date of death. The account holder usually needs to see the death certificate and a copy of the will (if any), and evidence of your identity and involvement before disclosing information.

It is usual for a will drawn up by a solicitor to be retained by the firm for safe-keeping. There is often a receipt or letter from the solicitor acknowledging the deposit of the will. Similarly, a will which was drawn up by a bank would be held by that bank, and there should be a document indicating that that is the case. If the original will was held by the deceased and is found among the deceased personal papers, it must be carefully looked after. It is surprising how many original wills are inadvertently destroyed when clearing the house and disposing of old papers and bills.

The Funeral

The funeral arrangements are not a matter for the executor or administrator, unless he or she is also the relative of the deceased who would normally make the arrangements. They are not part of the official duties of the executor or administrator. There has, however, been a case in which the court held that, in the event of a dispute about the disposal of the deceased's body, an executor can make the decision, even overriding the views of the family.

On the other hand, the bill for the funeral is a priority debt of the estate and may be paid as soon as it is received. If there is sufficient ready cash in the estate, that cash may be used. Some funeral directors offer a discount for payment within a certain time. If the deceased's cash is insufficient to pay the account, the personal representative may pay from his own resources, if he can afford to do so, to qualify for the discount offered, and reimburse himself from the estate when sufficient funds are available. Often, a bank or building society will release funds from the deceased person's account to pay the funeral bill before the grant of representation issues. The bank or building society usually pays the funeral director direct. The production of the will is usually sufficient to persuade the bank or building society to help in this way. Obviously, this is desirable, and enquiries should be made of account holders on receipt of the will.

Where there is severe financial difficulty in paying for the funeral, assistance may be obtained from the Benefits Agency towards the costs of burial or cremation.

A headstone or other memorial is not regarded as part of the funeral expenses, although it is allowed by Her Majesty's Revenue and Customs as a debt against the estate for inheritance tax purposes (see Chapter 4). Unless the residuary beneficiary agrees to this expense, it should not be incurred by the personal representative.

The cost of a "wake" or other "celebration" does not amount to a debt of the estate and cannot be deducted when calculating the value of the estate.

Assets

Distinguishing Joint Assets

The executor or administrator is concerned only with property which was held by the deceased in his or her sole name, not property held jointly with a spouse, civil partner or other person. All bank or building society accounts held by more than one person are held by them as "joint tenants" unless special arrangements were made at the time the account was opened. A joint account does not therefore form part of the estate and so cannot be disposed of by a will or under an intestacy. Consequently the cash in a joint account should not be counted among the assets of the deceased so as to form part of the estate.

Although most things can be owned jointly, Premium Bonds cannot. Nor can they be transferred to another person. On the death of the holder, the bonds, unless cashed in before, remain in the prize draw for one year, after which they are withdrawn from the draw and are no longer eligible for prizes. They must then be cashed and the cash paid to the beneficiary entitled either by virtue of a specific gift, or by a gift of residue or under the rules on intestacy. If the bonds are to remain in the draw, the National Savings and Investments office must be so informed. To cash them will require production of the grant.

Apart from premium bonds and individual savings accounts (ISAs), generally any type of savings account can be held in joint names, and unless other arrangements were made when the account was opened, at the death of one of the joint owners, the deceased owner's share passes automatically to the surviving joint owner(s). If you have any doubt whether an account is a joint account, simply ask the bank or building society concerned. As the account passes to the survivor, it can be transferred into the survivor's sole name on production of a copy death certificate; there is no need to produce the grant of representation.

The same principle applies to real property – the home usually – if it was owned in joint names. It forms part of the deceased's estate only if it does not automatically pass to a joint owner by survivorship on the death of the person whose estate is being dealt with. Most properties do in fact pass to the surviving owner. You can usually tell the type of ownership by reading the deeds. Words such as "joint tenants", "joint owners" or "joint holders" all signify a property passing by survivorship; "tenants in common" indicates the contrary.

If the deeds are not found in the house, they may be deposited at the deceased's bank, or, if the house is subject to a mortgage, they will be with the bank or building society which loaned the money. An enquiry of the bank or building society will elicit the type of ownership, and, if necessary, copies of extracts from the deeds can be requested. At the same time as making these enquiries, details of any outstanding mortgage, and whether such mortgage was covered by an endowment or other security insurance, should be obtained. The sooner insurance money is claimed to pay off the mortgage, the less interest accrues.

It is less likely that the house is owned as "joint tenants" if the owners are not husband and wife or civil partners. If the owners decided (usually at the time they bought the house) that their individual interests in the house should not pass to the survivor on the death of the first of them, the owners are said to hold the house as "tenants in common". The effect is that, on the death of one of the owners, the interest the deceased had in the property is part of his or her estate. What happens to it depends on the provisions of the will or the rules of intestacy, as appropriate. It is not transferred automatically to the surviving co-owner. The word "interest" here means that part of the property which is owned by each individual. This is usually fixed by the number of owners; if there are two owners, the interest of each individual is one half; three owners, one third and so on. But the property may be held in unequal shares or percentages. This will be clear from the deeds.

Sometimes solicitors or other financial advisers suggest that a joint tenancy be "severed", that is, changed to a tenancy in common. This splits the value of the property so that the shares individually held pass on each tenant's death, thus lessening the burden of tax payable on the death of the survivor. Again, if this has been done, it will be clear from the deeds. If the joint tenancy has not been severed it can be done after the death of a joint tenant, again to reduce a liability for inheritance tax. This must be done within two years of the date of death. Professional advice should be taken if this is contemplated.

Personal Chattels

Personal chattels are defined by law. The definition dates back to the Administration of Estates Act 1925 (section 55(i)(x)), but it is worth quoting since the meaning is quite clear:

> "carriages, horses, stable furniture and effects (not used for business purposes), motor cars and accessories (not used for business purposes), garden effects, domestic animals, plate, plated articles, linen, china, glass, books, pictures, prints, furniture, jewellery, articles of household or personal use or ornament, musical and scientific instruments and apparatus, wines, liquors and consumable stores".

Items such as TV sets, radios, personal computers, stereo equipment, i-pods and other appliances fall within the definition, but business assets are specifically excluded. So personal chattels includes anything of a personal nature, such as a bicycle or clothes.

If the deceased owned a car then, unless it was a vintage model or otherwise particularly valuable, it may be sold as long as it was not the subject of a specific gift in the will. The normal procedure for sale, giving the appropriate part of the vehicle registration document to the buyer, and notifying the Driver and Vehicle Licensing Centre in Swansea, should be carried out by the executor or administrator. The proceeds of sale should be held as part of the residuary estate. Until sale, and especially if the car is kept on the road, it must be insured and road tax must be paid. It is clear that any car should be disposed of quickly to avoid on-going expense to the estate.

Property Rented Out

If the deceased owned property which he or she had rented to someone else, the liability of the tenant to pay the rent continues after the owner's death. If the rent was being paid to an agent acting for the deceased, the agent may be instructed to continue collecting the rent until the future of the property is decided. In due course, it may be sold, or it may pass to a beneficiary who, once the property is transferred to him, may wish to make different arrangements. The agent's charges, if not deductible from the rent collected (although they usually are), are payable from the estate and should be paid when due by the executor or administrator. If no agent was employed, or if it is decided not to employ the agent any longer, then the tenant(s) should be told of the owner's death and asked to make the payments to you as the deceased's personal representative. Rent paid from the date of the deceased's death until final distribution of the estate attracts income tax, the payment of which is the personal representative's responsibility. The tax, together with any other debts, is deducted from the assets of the estate before distributing the estate (see pages 133–134).

Stocks and Shares and Unit Trusts
With the privatisation of many of the former public utilities and the flotation on the stock market of several former building societies, it is common for people to own stocks, shares or both.

Where the shareholdings are large or there are shares in a variety of different companies, or the shares are in a private company not quoted on the Stock Exchange, it may be simpler (and indeed cheaper in the end) to ask a stock broker for a valuation, at the date of death, of the shares in the quoted companies; and to approach the company secretaries concerned for a valuation of any unquoted shares. Any costs incurred in doing so are considered proper expenses and are recoverable out of the estate. Where the shares held are in one or two companies, a valuation may be calculated from the *Financial Times* for the day of the date of death. Many public libraries carry back editions of newspapers such as the *Financial Times*; they are also available on the internet.

Forms for the sale of quoted shares can often be obtained on request from the company registrar and are quite easy to complete. If the deceased had a substantial holding in a particular company, or had shares in a number of companies, it is advisable to obtain professional guidance and perhaps employ a stockbroker to sell the shares. Obviously it is in the interests of all beneficiaries for the best possible price to be obtained.

If the deceased invested in a unit trust or other investment trust, a valuation, together with details of any dividends or interest due, should be obtained from the fund manager.

Deceased's Personal Income
If the deceased was employed at the date of death or was receiving a private pension, the paying company must be told of his death and asked to calculate the pay or pension up to the date of death. Any money due is payable to the estate, and any overpayment is a

debt of the estate. Similarly, if the deceased was in receipt of a state pension or other state benefits the Department for Work and Pensions should be told of the death as soon as possible so that payments (now often paid automatically into a bank or building society account) can be stopped and any arrears or overpayment calculated. If, as is the case in the civil service and many other public service pension schemes, there was any arrangement for the pension, or a proportion of it, to become payable on death to a surviving spouse, civil partner or other nominated person, then the employer, or those who administer the pension fund, should be asked to make the appropriate arrangements.

Generally, the Department for Work and Pensions, employers and administrators of pension schemes (usually referred to as trustees) accept the death certificate or a copy of it as sufficient authority for them to make whatever payments are due on death. But if they will not act until the grant of representation is produced, then clearly nothing can be done until later when the grant becomes available. At least the correct figures are available, to calculate the estate's value. Likewise the trustees may require evidence of marriage or civil partnership, by production of the marriage or civil partnership certificate, before they make any payments to the surviving spouse or civil partner. Pension payments and lump sums payable by former employers on death are usually paid direct to the surviving spouse or civil partner, nominated next of kin or other nominated beneficiary, and the trustees correspond direct with him or her. Such payments do not usually form part of the estate.

Real Property
Real property – houses and land – may be difficult to value. Nevertheless, as accurate a valuation as possible must be obtained.

If it is quite clear that the total value of the estate will fall below the threshold for inheritance tax applicable at the date of death (£312,000 from 6 April 2008 – see Chapter 4) and that there is no likelihood that the estate will be liable for inheritance tax, then your own estimate of the value of the property, provided it is realistic, is sufficient. If you are in any doubt, then ask an estate agent for an informal valuation based on his knowledge of the area where the property is situated.

If the house is to be sold, there is no reason why it should not be placed on the market at this stage. A home information pack generally has to be drawn up, and this can take some time, so it as well to set the wheels in motion as soon as possible. The asking price recommended by the estate agent can be taken as the value of the property. The sale cannot be completed, however, until you have obtained the grant. It is usual to instruct a solicitor or licensed conveyancer to conduct the conveyancing process. You should tell that person that you are applying for a grant.

Where tax is likely to be payable, a formal valuation must be obtained, whether or not the house is to be sold. It may be that HM Revenue and Customs will ask the district valuation officer to inspect the property and fix its value. But this procedure is usually dispensed with if the property is to be sold in the near future. Here, HM Revenue and Customs usually accepts that the price for which the property is sold is its value. The asking price for the property should be used as the value for purposes of probate or administration. The value can be revised by telling HM Revenue and Customs when the actual selling price is known. Again, the property can be put on the market without delay, but completion of the sale cannot take place until you have the authority of the grant to sign the transfer.

If the property is not to be sold for some time, a valuation at the date of death will, of course, be required. It is this value which is used for probate purposes, but the eventual sale price may be used for tax purposes (any gain in value while the estate is being administered is subject to capital gains tax; see pages 134–135). If you are in doubt about whether a full valuation is necessary you should enquire of the probate registry to which you intend making your application (see page 75). The registry may refer you to HM Revenue and Customs for a final decision. Inheritance tax is discussed more fully in Chapter 4.

Protecting the Assets
It is worth mentioning here that the personal representative has a responsibility to protect the assets constituting the estate. For example, if a house is left empty, the executor or administrator should take reasonable steps to ensure its security and protect it from vandalism, perhaps informing the local police that the house is empty. Likewise, the personal representative must make sure the property and the contents are properly insured. Insurers must be told if the house is to be left vacant, as this affects the cover, and the

premium is likely to increase. Premiums due must be paid out of the funds of the estate. If there are insufficient funds, the premiums may be paid by you as the personal representative and reclaimed as part of your administration charge (see page 137).

Personal chattels or house contents which are the the subject of gifts should be given as soon as possible; see also Chapter 8. Arrangements for the disposal of other contents should be made, if only to minimise the risk of burglary.

It may be obvious, but it is worth mentioning that the water supply should be cut off and the heating and hot water systems drained to avoid damage by freezing if the house is left empty during the winter. Other precautions may also be necessary. Insurers usually insist on certain measures as a condition of cover. These steps must be taken or the insurance may lapse.

Where a property has been vacant or is likely to be vacant for longer than six months, the local authority can apply for an empty dwelling management order under the Housing Act 2004 – another reason why delay in disposal should be avoided.

Urgency
There are rare occasions where a grant of representation is needed urgently, before the value of the estate can be calculated, to deal with a particular asset. This might happen where the deceased had agreed to sell property, but died before the sale could be completed or if you have arranged a sale at an advantageous price but are not yet able to apply for a full grant. A special form of grant called an "ad colligenda bona" grant may be applied for to deal with this particular sale only. Advice on such applications may be obtained from the probate registry.

Nominated Property
A person may "nominate" another person to receive a particular item of property when the person making the nomination dies. For example, most people nominate their next of kin to receive any lump sum or pension payable by their employers. Savings certificates and Post Office accounts are also common examples. Such property is known as "nominated property". It does not form part of the estate, but passes directly to the person who has been nominated. Where there is doubt whether any savings were nominated, the organisation holding the money will advise. The

form you receive from the probate registry (Form IHT205) has a special place for nominated property to be entered (see page 99).

Estate Bank Account

It is advisable to open an executor's or administrator's account (the "estate account") with a bank or building society of your choice. It does not have to be the bank or building society where the deceased held an account, but it is sometimes easier administratively if they are the same. The bank might then, for example, in certain circumstances, transfer money to the estate account if it is required urgently for administration purposes.

It is wise to ask the bank or building society which type of account will give the estate the best return.

Any cash found at the deceased's house or in his or her wallet or handbag, and all money received by the estate, can be paid into this account. Bills can be paid from it, and payments made to the beneficiaries.

The account should be set up at an early stage, even before the grant has issued, so that cash can be deposited.

It is important to maintain an accurate record of all transactions (easily done with the help of the bank statements) and to avoid "mixing" estate money with your own. Regrettably, disputes do arise and it is better if everything is clearly "above board". If you are an executor, your authority to open the account comes from the will, not the grant of probate. If you are a proposed administrator, it is wise to consult any other person who is or may be entitled to apply for a grant of administration before opening the account, and agree with him or her that you will take the preliminary steps.

Usually, the assets (other than specific gifts of small intrinsic value and personal chattels) which constitute the estate cannot be sold or passed on to those who are to inherit them before the grant of representation has been issued. But, where there are assets which pass by survivorship to a surviving spouse or civil partner these should be transferred into the survivor's name as soon as possible. For example, a bank or building society account can be changed into the survivor's name by producing the death certificate to the bank or building society. The bank or society will take the necessary steps to change the name of the account.

Likewise, some asset holders may be prepared to pass on the assets they hold to the estate without the production of the grant. If this is possible, it should be done, and the money used to pay off any interest-accruing debt(s), the funeral account, or both. Some banks and building societies require an indemnity before they pay out funds in the absence of the authority of a grant of representation. This is to protect the asset holder against any claim that it made the payment wrongfully. The bank or building society usually provides a form of indemnity but often charges a fee for this service, which may exceed the £90 payable for a grant. In this case it may clearly be preferable to wait for the grant.

Liabilities

Having established what the deceased person owned, it is next necessary to trace all his or her debts, since these must, obviously, be paid off before the estate is shared out among the beneficiaries. The debts are also deducted from the value of the estate when calculating whether inheritance tax is payable.

Most people keep records of their financial transactions, and details of their personal affairs are often found with the will, although this is more likely to be true in respect of assets than liabilities.

The common household bills for gas, electricity and so on are easily identified. The gas, electricity and telephone companies should be told of the deceased's death. If the deceased person lived alone, the companies should be asked to make final meter readings. The local authority and water company should also be told of the death so that council tax and water rates accounts can be adjusted. Most people have mobile phones, so the service provider must be notified of the death and the account cancelled.

If the deceased had equipment, such as a television set, on hire, the rental company should be notified as soon as possible of the death, and arrangements made for the company to take back its property or transfer the rental arrangements to someone else. The same applies to goods on hire purchase. Such property does not belong to the deceased, but to the company which provided the finance. The estate is liable for any instalments due and unpaid at the date of death.

If the deceased had credit cards, debit cards or charge cards, the companies should be told of the death and asked for final statements. The cards should be destroyed unless the company asks for them back, in which case they should be cut in half before they are sent. Similarly, if the deceased had an account with a mail order company, that organisation should be informed and final account figures obtained. Newspapers and magazines should probably be cancelled, as should milk and anything else regularly delivered. Final accounts should be requested, and these may be paid out of any readily available cash. If the deceased had a passport, it should be returned to the Passport Office for cancellation and destruction.

Many of these points of course apply only where the deceased lived alone. Where he or she is survived by a spouse, child, friend or other cohabitee who may wish to keep the goods in question, then the relevant organisations should still be informed of the deceased's death, so that suitable new arrangements can be made and new accounts opened in the survivor's name.

If there is any doubt about the extent of the debts incurred by the deceased, it may be necessary to advertise for creditors. This may be done by placing an advertisement in the *London Gazette* (which is a publication where all types of public notices must by law be given), and a local newspaper circulating in the area where the deceased lived. The advertisement will ask any creditors to give details of any debt they say is owing. If it is thought the deceased might have incurred debts outside the area where he lived, for example, if he had a business in a different locality, it may be necessary to advertise in a newspaper circulating in that other area. Example advertisements are given below.

For a local newspaper

Re: JOHN SMITH deceased

Notice is hereby given pursuant to Section 27 of the Trustee Act 1925 that any person having a claim against or an interest in the estate of **JOHN SMITH** deceased, late of 1 The Avenue, Acaciaville, Loamshire, who died on 29 March 2008 is hereby required to send particulars in writing of his or her claim or interest to the undersigned not later than 30 June 2008 after which date the personal representatives will distribute the estate among the persons entitled thereto having regard only to the claims and interests of which they have had notice and will not, in respect of the estate so distributed, be liable to any person of whose claim they shall not have had notice.

Dated 17 April 2008
Signed (A Bloggs) of the Millstone, Pound Lane,
Bakerstone, Breadshire (Personal Representative)
To comply with the Act, the date by which claims are to be received
must be at least two months after the date of the advertisement.

For the London Gazette
The notice sent to the *London Gazette* must set out the information to
be published, strictly in the following order:
- deceased's name;
- address and occupation;
- date of death;
- name of person inserting the notice (name of personal
  representative);
- date by which notice must be received.

For example:

BLACKADDER Kevin Keith; The Millstone, Anytown,
Daleshire; author; 29 February 2008; Andrew Tinason,
The Nest, Anytown, Daleshire (Andrew Tinason); 30
August 2008.

The notice should be sent to the office of the London Gazette,
Atlantic House (Room B52), Holborn Viaduct, London EC1P 1BN,
and should be accompanied by a letter requesting that the notice be
inserted in the *Gazette* under "Notices pursuant to the Trustee Act
(notices for claims)". The letter should also request that a copy of
the published notice be sent to the personal representative. The
notice must be accompanied by the fee for the insertion, which
varies, so an enquiry by letter or telephone (020 7873 8300) should
be made in advance.

Checklists

There now follow lists of the most common assets and liabilities in
an estate; these can be used as checklists:

Assets	*Liabilities*
Cash: bank notes and coins	Household bills – gas, electricity, telephone
Cash in bank account(s)	Hire purchase commitments
Cash in building society account(s)	Income tax
	Council tax
Cash in Post Office savings account(s)	Mortgage repayments

Premium bonds
Insurance policy/ies
Pay/pension
House or flat
Contents of the home
Stocks/shares
Unit trusts
Tessas
ISAs

Personal loan repayments
Rent
Mail order accounts
Credit card accounts
Insurance premiums (for property or individual items of special value, such as jewellery)

Chapter 4

Inheritance Tax

Introduction

Inheritance tax was introduced in 1986. It replaced capital transfer tax, which itself had taken the place of estate duty in 1975. Inheritance tax is levied on the estate of a deceased person, and is sometimes still referred to as "death duty".

Inheritance tax is charged at the rate of 40 per cent of the value of the estate that exceeds a "nil rate band". This "nil rate band", the threshold at which tax becomes payable, is usually increased each year. It is presently £312,000, which applies in respect of deaths on or after 6 April 2008. For example, if a person dies in May 2008 with no reliefs available, and leaves an estate worth £350,000–

Value of estate...................... £350,000
Nil rate band........................ £312,000
Amount chargeable to tax......£38,000
Tax @ 40 per cent..................£15,200

The Chancellor of the Exchequer also set the thresholds (nil rate bands) to apply in subsequent tax years in the budget of 2007, and for 2009/10 the threshold will be £325,000.

The purpose of this chapter is to explain the principles of inheritance tax and to give brief guidance about the numerous exemptions and reliefs. A book of this nature clearly cannot provide a comprehensive guide to the intricacies of the tax. Anyone whose estate is likely to attract payment of tax is strongly advised to take professional advice from a solicitor, bank manager or accountant so that the estate can be disposed of to the best advantage and so as to avoid paying unnecessary tax. Indeed, one of the main reasons for making a will is to take advantage of inheritance tax concessions. Useful guidance is now available on the website of HM Revenue and Customs.

The way in which information about the value of the estate is given to HM Revenue and Customs, and how any tax due is calculated and paid, are dealt with in Chapter 5.

The Estate

There are many situations in which an estate qualifies as an "excepted estate", so that no inheritance tax is payable and a full inheritance tax account does not need to be prepared and submitted to HM Revenue and Customs. The regulations which deal with these situations are the Inheritance Tax (Delivery of Account) (Excepted Estates) Regulations 2004, and were last updated with effect from September 2006. The information set out below is current at the time of going to press (April 2008).

From 6 April 2004 there are three types of excepted estate:
- low value estates;
- exempt estates;
- estates of persons dying domiciled abroad

Low Value Estates
Low value estates are estates which do not give rise to a liability to inheritance tax because the gross value of the estate does not exceed the inheritance tax threshold applying at the date of death. An estate falls within this category if the following conditions are met:
- the deceased died domiciled in the United Kingdom;
- the gross value of the estate does not exceed the inheritance tax threshold;
- if the estate includes any assets in trust, they are held in a single trust and the gross value does not exceed £150,000;
- if the estate includes foreign assets, their gross value does not exceed £100,000;
- if there are any specified transfers, their chargeable value does not exceed £150,000;
- the deceased had not made a gift with reservation of benefit;
- the deceased did not have an alternatively secured pension fund, either as the original scheme member or as the

dependant or relevant dependant of the original scheme member.

Exempt Estates

Exempt estates are estates where there is no liability to inheritance tax because the gross value of the estate does not exceed £1 million and there is no tax to pay because one or both of the following exemptions (see page 73) apply:

- the spouse or civil partner exemption;
- the charity exemption.

No other exemption or relief can be taken into account. Spouse or civil partner exemption can be deducted only if both spouses or civil partners have always been domiciled in the United Kingdom. The charity exemption can be deducted only if the gift in question is an absolute gift to the charity concerned.

The conditions for these estates are that:

- the deceased died domiciled in the United Kingdom;
- the gross value of the estate does not exceed £1 million; and
- the net chargeable value of the estate after deduction of liabilities and spouse or civil partner exemption and/or charity exemption only does not exceed the inheritance tax threshold applying at the date of death;
- if the estate includes any assets in trust, they are held in a single trust and the gross value does not exceed £150,000 (unless the settled property passes to a spouse or civil partner or to a charity, when the limit is waived);
- if the estate includes foreign assets, their gross value does not exceed £100,000;
- if there are any specified transfers, their chargeable value does not exceed £150,000;
- the deceased had not made a gift with reservation of benefit; and
- the deceased did not have an alternatively secured pension fund, either as the original scheme member or as the dependant or relevant dependant of the original scheme member.

Persons Dying Domiciled Abroad

In the case of a person dying domiciled abroad, there is no liability to inheritance tax if the gross value of the estate in the United

Kingdom does not exceed £150,000. The conditions for these estates are that:

- the deceased died domiciled outside the United Kingdom;
- the deceased was never domiciled in the United Kingdom or treated as domiciled in the United Kingdom for inheritance tax purposes;
- the deceased's United Kingdom estate consisted only of cash or quoted shares and securities passing under a will or intestacy or by survivorship;
- the gross value of the estate did not exceed £150,000; and
- the deceased did not have an alternatively secured pension fund, either as the original scheme member or as the dependant or relevant dependant of the original scheme member.

Some technical terms are used in the above criteria. This is because the criteria are extracted from the regulations. For example, "domiciled in the United Kingdom" means that the deceased lived in the United Kingdom and was treated by HM Revenue and Customs as permanently residing here so that he paid income tax on his income here and did not qualify for any relief because he paid tax on income derived outside the United Kingdom. It is extremely unlikely the deceased was the recipient of an alternatively secured pension fund, but if he was, it is advisable to take advice from a solicitor or accountant.

When Tax is Payable

Inheritance tax is assessed on the value of the deceased person's estate. The common components of this "estate" for inheritance tax purposes include:

- *Free estate:* This is made up of everything that a person owns outright and which passes under the terms of a will or under the intestacy provisions on death. After death it is the responsibility of the executor or administrator to identify the estate (as explained in Chapter 3) and to administer it, as set out in Chapters 7 and 8.
- *Joint property:* As we have seen (pages 53–54) most assets – house, land, bank and building society accounts, household goods – can be owned jointly. Property which is held jointly with another person is liable for tax only to the extent of the

share held by the deceased person; that share forms part of the free estate and is liable to tax. If the deceased's property passes by survivorship, it does not count for inheritance tax purposes. If there is doubt whether property is held as a joint tenancy (where it passes by survivorship) or as a tenancy in common (where it is owned in defined shares), it may be necessary to take legal advice.

If the persons owning the property are husband and wife or civil partners, no tax is payable on property passing by survivorship, nor on the deceased's half share if the property is held as tenants in common and has been left to the surviving spouse or civil partner under the will, because no tax is payable on estate passing between husband and wife or civil partners. However, tax may be payable on the deceased's half share if the owners are not married or civil partners, or if the property is held as tenants in common and has not been left to a surviving spouse or civil partner. If the value of the half share, when aggregated with the remainder of the estate, exceeds the current threshold, tax is payable.

- *Nominated property:* In the case of some savings you are allowed to nominate who should receive the cash when you die, as explained on page 59. Even though it has been "nominated" in this way, this property still forms part of the estate for inheritance tax purposes.

- *Settled property:* Property can be given to trustees with instructions to pay the income arising from it (such as rent, if it is leased out to someone else) to a beneficiary – called the "life tenant" – for as long as he or she lives, and to give the property to other beneficiaries when the life tenant dies. Sometimes the life tenant does not receive income, but is entitled to live in the property instead. The property, or the house, is called "settled property". Although the life tenant does not fully own the settled property, he is treated as if he owned it for inheritance tax purposes. The value of the settled property therefore forms part of the estate of the life tenant when he or she dies.

- *Gifts with reservation:* A "gift with reservation" is a gift of property, made on or after 18 March 1986, which is not fully given away. A gift is a gift with reservation when either (a) the

69

person receiving the gift did not have real possession and enjoyment of the property; or (b) the person making the gift was excluded, or virtually excluded, from enjoyment of the property or did not retain any benefit either directly or indirectly from the gift. There is no seven year limit as there is for outright gifts (see *Potentially Exempt Transfers*, below).

A good example is the gift of a house where the donor continues to live in the house rent-free after he or she has transferred ownership to someone else. If the reservation (that is, in our example, the arrangement to live in the house rent-free) continues up to the date of death of the donor, the property is treated for inheritance tax purposes as if it forms part of the deceased's estate.

A gift may begin as a gift with reservation but some time later the reservation may cease, or a gift may start as an outright gift and then become a gift with reservation.

For example, if you give your house to your child but continue to live there rent-free, that would be a gift with reservation. If, after two years, you start to pay a market rent for living in the house, the reservation ceases when you first pay the rent. The gift then becomes an outright gift at that point and the seven year period (see *Potentially Exempt Transfers*, below) runs from the date the reservation ceased.

Again if you give your house to your child and continue to live there but pay full market rent, there is no reservation. If, over time, you stop paying rent or the rent does not increase, so it is no longer market rent, a reservation arises at the time the rent stops or ceases to be market rent.

Valuation of the Estate for Tax Purposes

The basis on which the estate is valued is the price the assets might reasonably be expected to fetch if sold on the open market at the date of death. We have already mentioned (page 58) the steps that may have to be taken to obtain a valuation of the deceased's real property.

For inheritance tax purposes, the value of the estate may be reduced by making the adjustments described below.

Agricultural Property

Agricultural property occupied for the purpose of agriculture can usually be reduced in value by 50 per cent or 100 per cent, depending on the circumstances.

Agricultural relief is due at 100 per cent if, immediately before the transfer, the transferor had the right to vacant possession of the property or the right to obtain it within the next twelve months, or

- land was let on a grazing licence;
- property is let on a tenancy beginning on or after 1 September 1995; or
- the transitional provisions for let property apply.

Relief is due at a lower rate of 50 per cent in any other case (principally where property is let on a tenancy granted before 1 September 1995 and the transitional provisions do not apply).

Agricultural relief has become extremely complex in the last few years because of changes in legislation (concerning milk quotas, for example) and many court cases on the interpretation of the legislation have been brought. If there is anything in the estate which could be regarded as "in agricultural use" specialist advice from a solicitor or accountant experienced in agricultural matters should be obtained.

Woodland

Reductions may be available for land which qualifies as woodland but does not qualify for agricultural relief.

Business Property

Business property, partnership interests and shares in companies that are not quoted on a recognised stock exchange usually qualify for a reduction in value of 100 per cent, depending on the circumstances.

If, within one year of the death, shares quoted on the Stock Exchange are sold for less than the value at the date of death, application may be made to adopt the sale price as the value for inheritance tax purposes.

Subject to certain conditions, when land or houses are sold within three years of the death for less than the value at the date of death, the sale price may be substituted as the value for inheritance tax purposes.

You should enquire at HM Revenue and Customs if you are in doubt about what reliefs are available. HM Revenue and Customs is at Ferrers House, PO Box 38, Castle Meadow Road, Nottingham NG2 1BB. All inquiries and communications concerning inheritance tax are dealt with by HM Revenue and Customs; the probate registries play no part in this. Questions about, for example, whether a full form of account for inheritance tax purposes is required (see page 80) are resolved between the personal representative(s) and HM Revenue and Customs.

All debts and liabilities of the estate due at the date of death may be deducted from the value of the estate. Reasonable funeral expenses, including the cost of a tombstone, are also allowed, but other costs of administering the estate may not be deducted from the value of the estate for inheritance tax purposes.

Potentially Exempt Transfers

Gifts made by a living person on or after 18 March 1986 are known as "potentially exempt transfers". In simple terms, a potentially exempt transfer is a gift from one living person to another. The gift will be exempt from inheritance tax if the person who made it lives for at least seven years after the date on which the gift was made. But if that person dies before the seven years expire, the exemption is lost or partially lost and tax may be payable. If the total of all potentially exempt transfers and any other chargeable transfers made in the seven years before death exceeds the threshold for inheritance tax, tax will be due. For example:

Potentially exempt transfer made 1 November
    2006 – chargeable value £250,000
Donor dies on 1 June 2008
Add chargeable value of other gifts in the
previous seven years £79,000
                                          £329,000
Deduct nil rate tax threshold at 1 June
    2008.. £312,000
Amount chargeable to tax £17,000
Tax @ 40 per cent... **£6,800**

To make matters worse, the personal nil rate band has been exhausted on the gifts made while the donor was alive; there is none left to set off against the value of the estate left on death.

Exemptions

A number of transactions are exempt from liability to inheritance tax. The following exemptions apply to potentially exempt transfers:

- a transfer of value to any one person not exceeding £250 in any twelve month period from 6 April to 5 April;
- the first £3,000 in value of transfers made in any twelve month period from 6 April to 5 April. If the exemption for the current year has been used up, then any exemption left over from the previous year may also be used;
- transfers comprising normal expenditure from income which do not affect the transferor's standard of living. Normal transfers must form part of a regular pattern of giving;
- a gift "in consideration of marriage or formation of a civil partnership" to a bride or groom or intended civil partner up to a limit of £5,000 from a parent; £2,500 from a bride, groom, intended civil partner or grandparent; or £1,000 from any other person;
- potentially exempt transfers made more than seven years before the death.

The following exemptions are generally available:

- all property passing between spouses and civil partners;
- transfers made to recognised charities established in the United Kingdom;
- gifts of land to (non-charitable) registered housing associations;
- transfers to specific institutions, for example, political parties represented in Parliament and other public bodies such as universities or the National Trust;
- transfers for national purposes to non-profit making organisations, with Treasury approval, of various kinds of property including land or buildings and objects of outstanding national, scientific or historical interest;
- where the deceased was a member of the armed forces or other listed body, and whose death was caused or hastened by service against the enemy or other warlike service (for example, serving in the armed forces in Iraq or Afghanistan);
- where the deceased person had a life interest in property that had been part of the estate of a predeceasing spouse who

died before 10 December 1974, the settled property is usually exempt.

Transfer of Remaining Nil-Rate Band

The Chancellor of the Exchequer announced in his Pre-Budget Report in October 2007 that, for deaths on or after 9 October 2007, it will be possible for surviving spouses and civil partners to claim the unused inheritance tax nil rate band allowance of a predeceased spouse or partner, no matter when the first person dies. At the time of going to press, the legislation to bring these provisions into force has not been enacted, but is to be included in the Finance Act 2008, to come into force in August 2008.

The claim to transfer unused nil-rate band must be made when the surviving spouse or civil partner dies, and not when the first of them dies. So if you are dealing with the estate of the first spouse or civil partner to die, there is nothing you need do now in terms of making a claim. However, you will need to record the proportion of the nil-rate band that goes unused. The detailed guidance issued by HM Revenue and Customs explains what sort of records must be kept in order to support a claim when the surviving spouse or civil partner dies.

If you are dealing with the estate of the surviving spouse or civil partner, you can make a claim to transfer the unused nil-rate band from the estate of the first spouse or civil partner to die. To make a claim, you will need to fill in a claim form, IHT216.

The form asks for information about the estate of the first spouse or civil partner to die, so that the amount of the nil-rate band that was unused can be calculated. You can then work out the amount to which the nil-rate band available to the survivor may be increased, and use that revised nil-rate band to calculate the inheritance tax payable on the survivor's estate. You should send the form to HM Revenue and Customs, together with the documents requested (for example, the death certificate of the first spouse or civil partner to die, a copy of that person's will and the marriage certificate) at the same time as you send form IHT200 for the estate of the survivor to HM Revenue and Customs. If you have any doubts or questions, they should be directed to HM Revenue and Customs.

More information on paying the tax is given on pages 114–115.

Chapter 5

Filling in the Forms

Which Court?

Before you go ahead with your application for a grant, a point to consider is which probate registry is most convenient for you. A list of probate registries, the sub-registries attached to them, and the probate offices run by each registry is on pages 151–153. For these purposes the Principal Registry in London can be considered to have the same function as a probate registry. There are no rules about which registry is appropriate; any registry can deal with any case. It is simply a matter of choosing the most convenient, bearing in mind that you will have to pay at least one visit there. Although called registries, these are in fact courts of law.

If there is more than one proposed applicant, generally speaking, they will all attend together. But where applicants live some distance apart, one of them may lodge the papers in the registry most convenient to him or her; that registry can then send the papers to another registry nearer the other applicant(s) so that he, she or they can attend there.

For simplicity, this chapter is again written as though there is only one applicant. If there is more than one, they must all sign the forms and undergo the same procedures.

You will note that no addresses or telephone numbers are given on pages 151–153 for the probate offices. This is because they run an "appointments only" system and, although personal callers will be seen, there may be a considerable wait if you have not made an appointment. Nor should you write to a probate office, since many of them are open only once or twice a month and your letter may languish undiscovered for a long time. Correspondence must be addressed to the main registry or sub-registry which runs the probate office to be sure it is dealt with promptly.

Obtaining the Forms

Several forms must be completed before applying for a grant, and most can be obtained by contacting the Probate and Inheritance Tax Helpline on 0845 302 0900, or doing what an increasing number of applicants are finding very convenient – obtaining them on-line at www.theprobateservice.gov.uk. You can also get the forms from your local registry or sub-registry. The forms will be the same regardless of your source. There is no charge for the forms.

What follows is a brief description of the forms (some of which are reproduced) and their uses. The form numbers are given, but as these change from time to time, it is a good idea to check the title of the form to make sure you have all you need. Again because of changes and up-dating, you may find there are subtle differences between the following descriptions and the forms you have. It is unlikely to be a fundamental change and the best thing to do is to complete the section in accordance with the guidance provided. There may also be additional inserts giving you up-to-date information on any recent changes, and it is a good idea to read them all before attempting to complete the forms.

Form PA1	Probate application form (reproduced on pages 85–88 and see page 77);
Form PA1a	Guidance Notes for Probate Application Form PA1;
Form PA2	Booklet entitled "How to Obtain Probate" (see page 78);
Form PA3	Probate Fees (see page 79);
Form PA4	Directory of Probate Registries and Interview Venues (see page 79);
Form PA6	My Probate Appointment – What Will Happen? (see page 78);
Form IHT205	HM Revenue & Customs Return of Estate Information (reproduced on pages 97–100 and see page 80);
Form IHT206	Notes to help you fill in form IHT205 (This form applies in respect of deaths on or after 1

September 2006. If the date of death in you.
application is earlier than this, please contact
HM Revenue & Customs on the helpline
number given above or on-line at
www.hmrc.gov.uk/cto

In addition, there is a form (IHT200) which is not available
from the probate registries. It has to be completed where a full
account of the estate for inheritance tax purposes is required. This
is explained later.

If you obtained your forms from a probate registry or sub-
registry, it is possible that an addressed envelope is included in the
package. It will be addressed to the registry from which you
obtained the forms, but this does not mean you are obliged to send
your completed papers to that registry.

It is sometimes possible to obtain forms from a Citizens' Advice
Bureau or law centre; some larger companies even have supplies in
their human resources or welfare offices departments. Forms
supplied by the Helpline, on-line or by the probate registries will be
those in current use, but forms obtained elsewhere may have been
around for some time and therefore may not be the latest versions.
This will not make the slightest difference to the validity of your
application, but could mean that some of the information given in
the explanatory material may not be current.

There now follows advice about how to complete the forms.
Examples of completed forms are set out at the end of this chapter.
Do not worry if you make a mistake; just cross it out and correct it.
Nearly everyone who completes the forms gets something wrong
and needs to make an amendment. As long as the form ends up
showing all the correct information, legibly, it is perfectly acceptable.

Form PA1: Probate Application Form

Form PA1 is known as the "instructions" form by the registries; it is
the document which gives details of you (the applicant for the
grant), the deceased, and the type of case. It is a blue and white
document, the white parts being those you complete. Each section
must be read carefully and the required details completed as fully as
possible. If there is some part of the form which you do not
understand, leave it blank, mention your doubts in a covering letter
to the registry and help will be provided. This advice applies to all

the forms, but it is especially important that this particular form should be completed accurately and as fully as possible because it is the basis of your application and the details it contains determine the form the application takes. An example of a completed form is given on pages 85–88.

Form PA1a: Guidance Notes for Probate Application Form PA1

This document is a quick guide to completing the form described above. It is designed to assist with the important parts of the form and there are several links (marked with an asterisk) which tie in with the PA1. There are also examples of the way in which the forms may be completed.

One point which is particularly important is the name of the person who has died. It is necessary to set out not only the person's true name, but also any other name in which, for example, assets were held or in which the will was made. It is by no means unusual for a will to be made in a slightly different name (often unused forenames are omitted) and it is important that all other names (known as "alias names") are identified. There is a section in this form which explains this in more detail and is well illustrated with examples.

Form PA2: How to Obtain Probate

You will note that you are advised to read booklet PA2 before completing Form PA1. This is good advice, although you will already have read similar information, in greater detail, in this book.

The booklet also contains information about the procedure to be followed after completing the forms. This is described more fully later in this chapter but, again, it is as well to read the relevant sections carefully. This applies equally to the rest of it. Although it is short (only some twelve pages), it is a mine of succinct information about the procedure and what you can expect once you have sent in the forms. It also contains useful advice on inheritance tax matters.

It concludes with a statement which should be borne in mind by all applicants. To paraphrase, once the grant has issued, the probate registry has discharged its responsibilities and cannot assist with the administration of the estate or answer any questions about it. If you find you are in difficulties or feel that matters have arisen which are complex, you should seek legal advice.

Form PA3: Personal Application Fees

Form PA3 is a list of the fees payable on personal applications. Further details about how and where the fees are to be paid are given on pages 111–112. Every effort is made to keep the list of fees up to date but changes may overtake what is printed. It is wise to use PA3 as a guide only, although you should look out for any note of a change which may be sent with the forms. The fees are reasonably straightforward and the fee for a personal application is now £90 unless the net estate is £5,000 or less, in which case there is no fee payable.

Form PA4: Directory of Probate Registries and Interview Venues

Form PA4 gives a list of all the probate registries and sub-registries, their addresses and days and times of opening and the names of the attached probate offices. The completed forms *must* be sent to the controlling registry or sub-registry, not to a probate office. Likewise, any contact with the registry must be made with the controlling registry and not direct with the probate office (see page 75).

Probate offices change location or even close altogether and it is impossible to keep reprinting the list, so this list is perhaps best taken as little more than a general guide to the whereabouts of the offices. In due course, you will have to visit the court in connection with your application and if this is to be at a local office, write its name in the space provided in Form PA1. If it turns out that the office has closed, you will be offered an appointment at the place nearest to your original choice. It should also be remembered that probate offices are open infrequently and you will get a quicker appointment at the main or sub-registry.

Form PA6: My Probate Appointment – What Will Happen?

The title says it all. Most people are concerned about attending the interview, and unsure what to expect. The idea behind this form is to put your mind at rest and at the same time answer those questions which are most often asked. The Probate Service understands what a stressful time this is and how daunting the thought of attending the court must be. The popular perception of being interviewed by an elderly man with a long white beard is as far from reality as can be. The interview, although important, is informal and designed to ensure the right person is applying for the grant. You will have to swear or affirm the truth of the document you have signed but this is necessary in every application. Please read PA6 before attending your interview; it will help.

Form IHT205: HM Revenue & Customs Return of Estate Information

This form is designed to save both you and the registry time. In certain circumstances, it is not necessary for the exact value of the estate to be shown in the grant, or for an account of the estate to be prepared and sent to HM Revenue and Customs. Form IHT205 is used to work out whether or not inheritance tax is likely to be payable and whether or not an account will have to be prepared for tax purposes. There is a full explanation on the form but, basically, if the total value of the estate does not exceed a certain sum (at present, £300,000) this may be what is called an "excepted estate" and it is likely that no account for HM Revenue and Customs will need to be prepared. In these circumstances, you need not complete Form IHT200, which will save you both time and trouble.

Complete all parts of IHT205 (there are good explanations of the terms) and if the total amount of the estate does not exceed £300,000 you need not complete Form IHT200. The sum of £300,000 is the appropriate sum when the date of death was 6 April 2007 or later; earlier than that and the figure is lower. On 6 August 2008, it will increase to £312,000.

The next part of the operation depends on whether or not you need to complete Form IHT200. The next chapter sets out the procedure, to which you can move on straight away if you do not need to complete Form IHT200. But if you find, having completed Form IHT205, that you do need to complete Form IHT200, you should telephone the Probate and Inheritance Tax Helpline on 0845 302 0900 requesting Form IHT200. This form is available from HM Revenue and Customs only (and can be completed on-line at www.hmrc.gov.uk), not from the probate registry or sub-registry.

Form IHT200: HM Revenue and Customs Account for Inheritance Tax

The notes which accompany Form IHT200 are comprehensive and the form has been designed to be as "user-friendly" as possible. If you follow the notes, you should have no trouble completing the form. An example of a completed form IHT 200 is reproduced on pages 89–96. It can also be filled in on-line at www.hmrc.gov.uk and printed out.

With Form IHT200, you will also receive Form D18 ("Probate summary", reproduced on page 110), which must be completed, together with several other forms which may or may not be relevant but should be used if necessary. You will also get form IHT19 ("Delivery of a reduced inheritance tax account") which is a guide to deciding whether the estate is an excepted estate (see above) and if it is not, whether you can complete a reduced form IHT200. Reading this may save you a great deal of time.

The explanatory notes (IHT210) are sent with IHT200 and are comprehensive, although a few hints of the authors' own are set out below.

Firstly, having made notes of the assets which comprise the deceased's estate, make sure you have been sent all the supplementary papers you need.

Care must be taken to answer all the questions. If there is no asset of a type referred to on the form, enter a zero or a dash. Failure to complete the form properly will delay the application and may mean that the form has to be returned.

Asset values: The values to be inserted are those for which the assets would have sold in the open market on the day of the deceased's death. Those values should be rounded down to the nearest £1. Actual values must be used and provisional estimates applied only in very special circumstances, for example in respect of foreign assets or income from a trust. No supporting evidence need be provided at this stage.

In Section A, you should enter the name of the registry or sub-registry (not the probate office) to which you have applied, or intend to apply.

Section B deals with the details of the deceased – name, dates of birth and death, address, and so on. The only questions which might cause concern are B14 (domicile), B16 (National Insurance number) and B18 (income tax reference). The deceased's domicile is crucial, not only for tax purposes but for the probate application. The probate registry's jurisdiction is based on domicile. Everyone has a domicile of origin but can change that domicile by habitually living in another country with an intention to stay there for ever. Remember that Scotland, Northern Ireland, the Channel Islands and the Isle of Man have their own systems of law and are regarded as "foreign" countries. Generally, the answer to the question is England and Wales.

The deceased's National Insurance number is to be found on any pension book (if the deceased person had retired) or payslip (if he or she was employed); and the tax reference appears on any letter from HM Revenue and Customs, coding notice or tax return.

Section C is about you, the applicant. It is important to HM Revenue and Customs (and the probate registry) to have a daytime telephone number. The staff of each organisation are forbidden to discuss personal details with any other person. This is especially so in respect of the deceased's tax affairs.

Section D is a series of tick boxes referring to additional forms relating to separate parts of the estate. The "D" forms, or "supplementary pages" are colour coded to match the boxes in this section. Booklet SP2 contains a complete list of the forms and the explanatory notes, and is sent with the forms pack.

Fill in Form D1 if the deceased left a will: a copy of the will must be sent to HM Revenue and Customs with the form (See the example on page 101)

Form D3 deals with gifts and transfers of values. Booklet SP2 explains exactly what is meant by a "gift", but if you are not certain you can always contact the Helpline at the above number.

D4 deals with joint assets, such as bank accounts and property held in the joint names of the deceased and another or others. It also deals with nominated assets. These assets have been discussed at page 53–54. A completed form D4 is shown on page 102.

If there were any assets held in trust, complete D5. Assets held in trust are, for example, income from a fund, rent, or where someone is allowed to live in a house free of rent and able to use the contents without charge as part of a trust gift.

Complete D6 in respect of any personal pension and give details of any lump sum payment due on death.

D7 must be completed with details of all stocks and shares held.

You will need to complete D9 if the deceased made regular payments or lump sum payments for life assurance or annuities.

In D10, details of household and personal goods must be set out. These are often difficult to value, but remember that some "second hand" goods are valueless. It is important not to overvalue these items. Please see pages 104–107 for an example of how to complete this form.

Form D10A is similar to form D10 but refers to household and personal goods given to charity.

You should use form D12 to set out details of any land or buildings the deceased may have owned, or any interest in land or buildings he/she may have had. A completed form is shown on pages 108–109.

Form D17 should be completed if there is any additional information which you should tell HM Revenue and Customs, but for which there is no space elsewhere on the previous forms.

Form D18 is the form which is of the greatest interest to the probate registries. This is the form which is stamped by HM Revenue and Customs and forwarded to the registry as proof that any inheritance tax due has been paid, or that none is payable. If a D18 is necessary, the grant cannot issue until it has been seen and stamped by HM Revenue and Customs and returned to the probate registry where your application for the grant has been made. Please see page 110.

You may find form D19 ("Confirmation that no inheritance tax is payable") useful if the estate does not attract inheritance tax.

Form 20 is an application form used to transfer funds to pay inheritance tax from accounts held by the deceased. This may not be possible in all situations, but it is a useful alternative to taking out a loan.

Section E applies to persons dying domiciled in Scotland.

Complete section F with the actual values of all the assets upon which payment of tax cannot be deferred. The list, F1 to F23, is comprehensive. Where there is no asset of the type described, insert a zero or a dash. The remainder of section F (on page 4) deals with liabilities (debts), funeral expenses, exemptions and reliefs.

Section G is for those assets on which any tax due may be paid by instalments. Details of exemptions and reliefs must be set out to provide the total chargeable value of assets.

Section H is a summary of the previous sections, which can be used in the calculation of the liability for inheritance tax, and section J is where the amount of tax payable is calculated.

Section K should be completed to show to whom any refund should be paid in the event of an overpayment.

Section L is the declaration which needs to be signed by you and which confirms the accuracy of the information you have supplied.

The forms supply the information to HM Revenue and Customs to enable them to calculate the amount of inheritance tax payable. However, it is possible for you to do that and thereby save time and make the administration of the estate easier. By completing form IHT200 (WS), you will be able to work out the inheritance tax payable and submit this to HM Revenue and Customs when you send in the forms. This will enable the forms to be processed more quickly and at the same time allow you a better overview of the estate and its liabilities. You will also be supplied with an comprehensive booklet (IHT123) which explains in detail how you can use this most useful form.

Examples of Completed Forms

Form PA1: Probate Application Form

Probate Application Form - PA1

Please use **BLOCK CAPITALS**

Name of deceased	JOHN EDWARD DOE
Interview venue	HARLOW
Dates to avoid	15 – 27 MAY, 18 JUNE

Please read the following questions and PA2 booklet 'How to obtain probate' carefully before filling in this form.
Please also refer to the Guidance Notes enclosed where an item is marked ".

PLEASE COMPLETE ALL SECTIONS.

Section A: The Will / Codicil

This column is for official use

*A1 Did the deceased leave a will/codicil?
(Note: These may not necessarily be formal documents. If the answer to question 1 is Yes, you must enclose the **original** document(s) with your application.)

Will: Yes ✓ No ☐   Codicil: Yes ☐ No ✓

If **No** to both questions, please go to Section B

Date of will

A2 Did the deceased marry or enter into a Civil Partnership after the date of the will/codicil? Yes ☐ Date: No ✓

Date of codicil

A3 Is there anyone under 18 years old who receives anything in the will/codicil? Yes ✓ No ☐

A4 Did any of the witnesses to the will or codicil or the spouse/civil partner of any witness receive a gift under the will/codicil? If Yes, state name of witness. Yes ☐ No ✓

A5 Are there any executors named in the will/codicil? Yes ✓ No ☐

*A6 Give the names of those executors who are **not** applying and the reasons why
Note: All executors **must** be accounted for.

Full names	Reason A,B,C,D,E
ALAN DOE	A
PHILIP DOE	D

A = Pre-deceased
B = Died after the deceased
C = Power Reserved
D = Renunciation
E = Power of Attorney

*B1 - B6 Please refer to the Guidance Notes.

Section B: Relatives of the deceased

Sections B1 - B4 must be completed in all cases.

Please state the **number** of relatives of the deceased in categories B1 - B4.

If there are no relatives in a particular category, write 'nil' in each box and move onto the next category.

Note: Sections B5 and B6 only need to be completed if the deceased had no relatives in Section B1 - B4.

Number of relatives (if none, write nil)	Under 18	Over 18
B1 Surviving **lawful** husband or wife or surviving **lawful** civil partner	nil	nil
B2a Sons or daughters who survived the deceased	nil	2
b Sons or daughters who did **not** survive the deceased	nil	nil
c Children of person(s) indicated at '2b' **only** who survived the deceased *		
B3 Parents who survived the deceased	nil	nil
B4a Brothers or sisters who survived the deceased	nil	nil
b Brothers or sisters who did **not** survive the deceased	nil	nil
c Children of person(s) indicated at '4b' **only** who survived the deceased *		
B5 Grandparents who survived the deceased		
B6a Uncles or aunts who survived the deceased		
b Uncles or aunts who did **not** survive the deceased		
c Children of person(s) indicated at '6b' **only** who survived the deceased *		

PA1 - Probate Application Form (01.07)   HMCS

		Section C: Details of applicant(s)	This column is for official use
Please note that the grant will normally be sent to the first applicant. Any applicant named will be required to attend an interview. It is, however, usually only necessary for one person to apply (please see PA2 booklet, page 3).			
C1	Title	Mr ✓ Mrs ☐ Miss ☐ Ms ☐ Other ☐	I.T.W.C
C2	Forenames	PAUL MICHAEL	
C3	Surname	DOE	
C4	Address	4 THE CRESCENT ANYTOWN LOAMSHIRE Postcode: A21 2XY	
C5	Telephone number	Home 01573 859000 Work 020 700 45678	
	E-mail address (optional)	paul@hopeful.com.uk	
C6	Occupation	PROPERTY DEVELOPER	
C7	Are you related to the deceased?	Yes ✓ No ☐	
	If Yes, what is your relationship?	Relationship: SON	
C8	If there are any other applicants, up to a maximum of three, give their details. (Note: **All** applicants named in Sections C1 and C8 must attend an interview.)	Details of other applicants who wish to be named in the grant of representation. (Please give details as C1 to C7 including relationship to deceased.) JENNIFER ALICE DOE 4 THE CRESCENT ANYTOWN LOAMSHIRE A21 2XY	
C9	Name and address of any surviving lawful husband or wife/civil partner of the deceased, unless stated above.	NONE Postcode:	
*C10	If you are applying as an attorney on behalf of the person entitled to the grant, please state their name, address and capacity in which they are entitled (e.g. relationship to the deceased).	Postcode: Relationship:	
C10a	Has the person named in section C10 signed an Enduring Power of Attorney?	Yes ☐ No ☐	
C10b	If Yes, has it been registered with the Public Guardianship Office?	Yes ☐ No ☐	

Section D: Details of the deceased	This column is for official use

*D1 Forenames — JOHN EDWARD

*D2 Surname — DOE

True name

*D3 Did the deceased hold any assets **(excluding joint assets)** in another name? — Yes ☐ No ☑

Alias

*D4a If Yes, what are the assets?

And in what name(s) are they held?

Address

D4b Was the deceased known by any other name in which he/she made a will? If so, what name was it made in? — Yes ☑ No ☐

JOHN DOE – MADE HIS WILL

D5 Last permanent address of the deceased.

27 THE DRIVE
HOMETOWN
ANYSHIRE

Postcode: HT27 5ZA

D/C district and No.

D6 Date of birth — 27/06/1924

D7 Date of death — 19/04/2007 — Age: 82

L.S.A.

Domicile

*D8 Was England and Wales the domicile/ permanent home of the deceased at the date of death? If No, please specify the deceased's permanent home or domicile. — Yes ☑ No ☐

D.B.F.

*D9 Tick the last **legal** marital or civil partnership status of the deceased, and give dates where appropriate.

Bachelor/Spinster ☐
Widow/Widower/Surviving Civil Partner ☑
Married/Civil Partnership ☐ Date:
Divorced/Civil Partnership dissolved ☐ Date:
Judicially separated ☐ Date:

Note: These documents (♦) may usually be obtained from the Court which processed the divorce/dissolution of civil partnership/separation.

*(If the deceased did **not** leave a will, please enclose official copy♦ of the Decree Absolute/Decree of Dissolution of Civil Partnership/Decree of Judicial Separation (as applicable))*

*D10 Was the deceased legally adopted? — Yes ☐ No ☑

*D11 Has any relative of the deceased been legally adopted? (If Yes, give name and relationship to deceased.) — Yes ☐ No ☑

Name:
Relationship:

D12 *Answer this section **only** if the deceased died **before 4th April 1988 or left a will or codicil dated before that date**.*

D12a Was the deceased illegitimate? — Yes ☐ No ☐

D12b Did the deceased leave any illegitimate sons or daughters? — Yes ☐ No ☐

D12c Did the deceased have any illegitimate sons or daughters who died leaving children of their own? — Yes ☐ No ☐

Important - please complete the checklist overleaf before submitting your application

Important

Checklist

Please return your forms to the probate registry which controls the interview venue at which you wish to be interviewed (see PA4) otherwise your application may be delayed.

Before sending your application, please complete this checklist to confirm that you have enclosed the following items:

1	PA1 (Probate Application Form)	✓
2	Either IHT205 (signed by all applicants)	✓
	or D18	
	Note: Do not enclose IHT Form 200 — **this must be sent to HMRC (Inheritance Tax)** (see PA2)	
3	Original will and codicil(s), **not a photocopy**	✓
	Note: Do not remove or attach anything to the will/codicil	
4	Official copy of death certificate or coroner's letter, **not a photocopy**	✓
5	Other documents as requested on PA1 — please specify	
6	Please state number of official copy grants required for use in England and Wales (see PA3)	4
7	Please state number of official copy grants required for use **outside** England and Wales (see PA3)	**For official use only (sealed and certified)**
8	Please state total amount of cheque enclosed for fee (made payable to HMCS) including cost for the number of official copy grants stated in 6 and 7 above.	£ 94.00

Note: If you do not enclose all the relevant items, your application may be delayed.

PLEASE ENSURE THAT ALL INFORMATION GIVEN IS ACCURATE AND THAT YOU KEEP COPIES OF ALL DOCUMENTS SENT

Official Use Only

Type of grant:

Power reserved to _____ [Name of executor/s]

Will message: with a codicil / and _____ codicils (delete as appropriate)

Limitation _____

Min interest   Yes / No

Life interest   Yes / No

Figures:- DNE / amounts to   Gross: £

                     Net: £   Fee paid: £

Clearing:-

Title:-

Footnote:-

Form IHT200: Inheritance Tax Account

HM Revenue & Customs

Inheritance Tax Account

Fill in this account for the estate of a person who died on or after 18 March 1986.
You should read the related guidance note(s) before filling in this form.
The notes follow the same numbering as this form for ease of reference.

A Write in the name of the Probate Registry, Commissary Court or Sheriff Court District where you will apply for a grant

A1 Principal   Date of grant

B Provide the following information about the person who has died

Title B1 MR   Surname B2 DOE

Other name(s) B3 JOHN EDWARD

Date of birth B4 27/06/1924   Date of death B5 19/04/2007

Marital or civil partnership status   Write whichever is appropriate a, b, c or d in the box B6 d
a married or in civil partnership b single c divorced or former civil partner d widowed or surviving civil partner

Last known permanent address

B7 27 THE DRIVE
HOMETOWN
ANYSHIRE

Postcode HT27 5ZA

Is B7 a care home?   B13 Yes   No ✓

Domicile   B14 ENGLAND & WALES

Occupation   B15 RETIRED

Surviving relatives

Spouse or civil partner B8 ✓

Brother(s)/sister(s) B9 ✓

Parent(s) B10

Number of children B11 2

Number of grandchildren B12 5

National insurance number B16 A B 1 2 3 4 0 1 2

Income tax district B17 TY GLAS, CARDIFF

Income tax or self assessment reference B18 123/A789

Did the deceased grant a power of attorney? B19 Yes   No ✓

C If you want us to deal directly with a solicitor or other person provide the following information about them

Name and address of firm or person dealing with the estate
C1

Postcode

DX number and town
C2 DX

Contact name and reference
C3

Telephone number
C4

Fax number
C5

IHT 200   www.hmrc.gov.uk/cto   Helpline 0845 30 20 900   HMRC CT 08/06

D Supplementary pages

You must answer all of the questions in this section, by ticking the box that applies.

If you answer "Yes" to a question you will need to fill in the supplementary page shown. If you do not have all the supplementary pages you need you can download them from the internet (www.hmrc.gov.uk/cto) or request them from the orderline: e-mail (hmrc.ihtorderline@gtnet.gov.uk) or telephone 0845 30 20 900.

		No	Yes	Page
• The Will	Did the deceased leave a Will?		✓	D1
• Domicile outside the United Kingdom	Was the deceased domiciled outside the UK at the date of death?	✓		D2
• Gifts and other transfers of value	Did the deceased make any gift or any other transfer of value on or after 18 March 1986 (including gifts with reservation and gifts involving previously owned assets)?	✓		D3
• Joint assets	Did the deceased hold any asset(s) in joint names with another person?		✓	D4
• Nominated assets	Did the deceased, at any time during their lifetime, give written instructions (usually called a "nomination") that any asset was to pass to a particular person on their death?	✓		D4
• Assets held in trust	Did the deceased have any right to any benefit from any assets held in trust or in a settlement at the date of death?	✓		D5
• Pensions	Did the deceased have a pension provision for retirement other than the State Pension?	✓		D6
• Stocks and shares	Did the deceased own any stocks or shares?	✓		D7
• Debts due to the estate	Did the deceased lend any money, either on mortgage or by personal loan, that had not been repaid by the date of death?	✓		D8
• Life insurance and annuities	Did the deceased pay any premiums on any life insurance policies or annuities which are payable to either the estate or to someone else or which continue after death?	✓		D9
• Household and personal goods	Complete form D10 in all cases. If the deceased did not own any household goods or personal possessions or they do not have any value, explain the circumstances on form D10.		✓	D10
• Interest in another estate	Did the deceased have a right to a legacy or a share of an estate of someone who died before them, but which they had not received before they died?	✓		D11
• Land, buildings and interests in land	Did the deceased own any land or buildings in the UK?		✓	D12
• Agricultural relief	Are you deducting agricultural relief from the value of any farm or farmland owned by the deceased?	✓		D13
• Business interests	Did the deceased own all or part of a business or were they a partner in a business?	✓		D14
• Business relief	Are you deducting business relief?	✓		D14
• Foreign assets	Did the deceased own any assets outside the UK?	✓		D15
• Debts owed by the estate	Are you claiming a deduction against the estate for any money that the deceased had borrowed from relatives, close friends, or trustees, or other loans, overdrafts or guarantee debts?	✓		D16

90

E **Domicile in Scotland - entitlement to claim legal rights**

Scottish legal rights entitlement (jus relicti/æ and or legitim) is relevant to this estate? No Yes

How many children are   under 18 ☐   18 and over ☐

F **Estate in the UK where tax may not be paid by instalments**

		Open market value at the date of death
• Quoted stocks, shares and investments *(box SS1, form D7)*	F1	0
• UK Government and municipal securities *(box SS2, form D7)*	F2	0
• Unquoted stocks, shares and investments	F3	0
• Traded unquoted stocks and shares	F4	0
• Dividends or interest	F5	0
• Premium Bonds *(including the value of any unclaimed or uncashed prizes)*	F6	£10,000
• National Savings investments *(show details on form D17, or Inventory form C1 in Scotland)*	F7	£7,893
• Bank and building society accounts *(list each account or investment separately on form D17, or Inventory form C1 in Scotland)*	F8	£52,175
• Cash	F9	£200
• Debts due to the deceased and secured by mortgage *(box DD1, form D8)*	F10	0
• Other debts due to the deceased *(box DD1, form D8)*	F11	0
• Rents due to the deceased, but unpaid at the date of death *(Include the property itself on form D12)*	F12	0
• Accrued income	F13	0
• Apportioned income	F14	0
• Other income due to the deceased *(box IP4, form D9, box PA1 form D6)*	F15	0
• Life insurance policies *(box IP3, form D9)*	F16	0
• Payments due to the deceased under private medical insurance to cover hospital or health charges incurred before death.	F17	0
• Income tax or capital gains tax repayment	F18	0
• Household and personal goods *(sold, box HG18, form D10)*	F19	£7,000
• Household and personal goods *(unsold, box HG17, form D10)*	F20	£15,000
• Interest in another estate unpaid at the date of death *(box UE1, form D11)*	F21	0
• Interest in expectancy *(reversionary interest)*	F22	0
• Other personal assets in the UK *(show details on form D17, or Inventory form C1 in Scotland)*	F23	0
Total assets *(sum of boxes F1 to F23)*	F24	£92,268

Liabilities, funeral expenses, exemptions and reliefs

- Liabilities incurred by the deceased before the date of death

Name	Description of liability	
MASTERCARD	CREDIT CARD	£293
VISA	STORE CARD	£105

Total liabilities *(write in the total of the items listed above)* **F25** £398

- Funeral expenses

A MOURNER & SON	£2,950

Total funeral expenses *(write in the total of the items listed above)* **F26** £2,950

Total liabilities and funeral expenses
(box F25 plus box F26. If box F27 is more than box F24 see explanatory notes) **F27** £3,348

Net total of assets less liabilities *(box F24 less box F27)* **F28** £88,920

- Exemptions and reliefs

Total exemptions and reliefs *(write in the total of the items listed above)* **F29** £0

Chargeable value of assets in the UK where tax may not be paid by instalments
(box F28 less box F29. Copy this figure to box WS1 on form IHT200WS) **F30** £88,920

G Estate in the UK where tax may be paid by instalments

Do you wish to pay the tax on these assets by instalments? *(Tick appropriate box)*   No ☐   Yes ☑

Interests in land owned by the deceased at the date of death

		Open market value at the date of death
• Deceased's residence *(excluding farm houses)*	G1	£750,000
• Other residential property	G2	
• Farms, farmland, farm buildings and farmhouses.	G3	
• Business property *(from which the deceased ran a business alone or in partnership)*	G4	
• Timber and woodland which is not part of a farm.	G5	
• Other land, buildings and rights over land	G6	

	Interest in a business	Interest in a partnership		
• Farming business	G7.1	G7.2	G7	£0

	Interest in a business	Interest in a partnership		
• Other business interests	G8.1	G8.2	G8	£0

	Farm trade assets	Other business assets		
• Business assets	G9.1	G9.2	G9	£0

• Quoted shares and securities, control holding only	G10	

	Control holding	Non-control holding		
• Unquoted shares	G11.1	G11.2	G11	£0

	Control holding	Non-control holding		
• Traded unquoted shares	G12.1	G12.2	G12	£0

Total assets *(sum of boxes G1 to G12)*	G13	£750,000

Liabilities, exemptions and reliefs *(that relate to the assets described in this section).*

• Name and address of mortgagee

G14	

• Other liabilities

Total of other liabilities G15	£0
Net total of assets less liabilities *(box G13 less boxes G14 and G15)* G16	£750,000

• Exemptions and reliefs

Total exemptions and reliefs G17	£0

Chargeable value of assets in the UK where tax may be paid by instalments *(box G16 less box G17)*   G18   £750,000

H **Summary of the chargeable estate**

You should fill in form IHT200WS so that you can copy the figures to this section and to section J. If you are applying for a grant without the help of a solicitor or other agent and you do not wish to work out the tax yourself, leave this section and section J blank. Go on to section K. The corresponding box numbers from the IHT200WS are shown in *italics*.

Assets where tax may not be paid by instalments

- Estate in the UK *(box WS1)* — **H1**
- Joint property - passing by survivorship *(box WS2)* — **H2**
- Foreign property *(box WS3)* — **H3**
- Settled property on which the trustees would like to pay tax now *(box WS4)* — **H4**

  Total of assets where tax may not be paid by instalments *(box WS5)* — **H5**

Assets where tax may be paid by instalments

- Estate in the UK *(box WS6)* — **H6**
- Joint property - passing by survivorship *(box WS7)* — **H7**
- Foreign property *(box WS8)* — **H8**
- Settled property on which the trustees would like to pay tax now *(box WS9)* — **H9**

  Total of assets where tax may be paid by instalments *(box WS10)* — **H10**

Other property taken into account to calculate the total tax

- Settled property *(box WS11)* — **H11**
- Alternatively secured pension *(box WS11A)* — **H11A**
- Gift with reservation *(box WS12)* — **H12**

  Chargeable estate *(box WS13)* — **H13**

  Cumulative total of lifetime transfers *(box WS14)* — **H14**

  Aggregate chargeable transfer *(box WS15)* — **H15**

J **Calculating the tax liability**

Calculating the total tax that is payable

- Aggregate chargeable transfer *(box WS16)* **J1**
- Tax threshold *(box WS17)* **J2**
- Value chargeable to tax *(box WS18)* **J3**

Tax payable *(box WS19)* **J4**

- Tax (if any) payable on lifetime transfers *(box WS20)* **J5**
- Relief for successive charges *(box WS21)* **J6**

Tax payable on total of assets liable to tax *(box WS22)* **J7**

Calculating the tax payable on delivery of this account

- Tax which may not be paid by instalments *(box TX4)* **J8**
- Double taxation relief *(box TX5)* **J9**
- Interest to be added *(box TX7)* **J10**

Tax and interest being paid now which may
not be paid by instalments *(box TX8)* **J11**

- Tax which may be paid by instalments *(box TX12)* **J12**
- Double taxation relief *(box TX13)* **J13**
- Number of instalments being paid now **J14** / 10 *(box TX15)*
- Tax now payable *(box TX16)* **J15**
- Interest on instalments to be added *(box TX17)* **J16**
- Additional interest to be added *(box TX18)* **J17**

Tax and interest being paid now which may be paid by instalments *(box TX19)* **J18**

Total tax and interest being paid now on this account *(box TX20)* **J19**

K **Authority for repayment of inheritance tax**

In the event of any inheritance tax being overpaid the payable order for overpaid tax and interest in connection with this estate should be made out to

PAUL M DOE

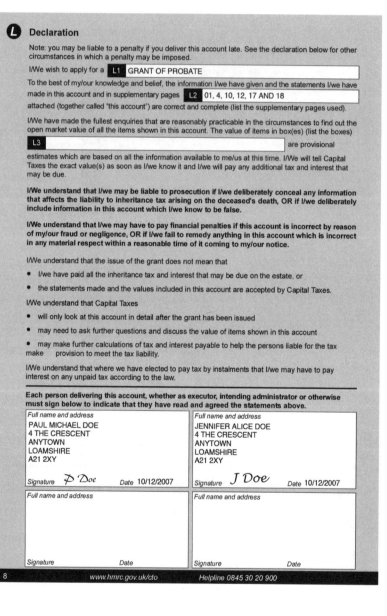

L **Declaration**

Note: you may be liable to a penalty if you deliver this account late. See the declaration below for other circumstances in which a penalty may be imposed.

I/We wish to apply for a **L1** GRANT OF PROBATE

To the best of my/our knowledge and belief, the information I/we have given and the statements I/we have made in this account and in supplementary pages **L2** 01, 4, 10, 12, 17 AND 18

attached (together called "this account") are correct and complete (list the supplementary pages used).

I/We have made the fullest enquiries that are reasonably practicable in the circumstances to find out the open market value of all the items shown in this account. The value of items in box(es) (list the boxes)

L3   are provisional

estimates which are based on all the information available to me/us at this time. I/We will tell Capital Taxes the exact value(s) as soon as I/we know it and I/we will pay any additional tax and interest that may be due.

I/We understand that I/we may be liable to prosecution if I/we deliberately conceal any information that affects the liability to inheritance tax arising on the deceased's death, OR if I/we deliberately include information in this account which I/we know to be false.

I/We understand that I/we may have to pay financial penalties if this account is incorrect by reason of my/our fraud or negligence, OR if I/we fail to remedy anything in this account which is incorrect in any material respect within a reasonable time of it coming to my/our notice.

I/We understand that the issue of the grant does not mean that

- I/we have paid all the inheritance tax and interest that may be due on the estate, or

- the statements made and the values included in this account are accepted by Capital Taxes.

I/We understand that Capital Taxes

- will only look at this account in detail after the grant has been issued

- may need to ask further questions and discuss the value of items shown in this account

- may make further calculations of tax and interest payable to help the persons liable for the tax make   provision to meet the tax liability.

I/We understand that where we have elected to pay tax by instalments that I/we may have to pay interest on any unpaid tax according to the law.

Each person delivering this account, whether as executor, intending administrator or otherwise must sign below to indicate that they have read and agreed the statements above.

Full name and address	Full name and address
PAUL MICHAEL DOE 4 THE CRESCENT ANYTOWN LOAMSHIRE A21 2XY	JENNIFER ALICE DOE 4 THE CRESCENT ANYTOWN LOAMSHIRE A21 2XY
Signature *P Doe* Date 10/12/2007	Signature *J Doe* Date 10/12/2007
Full name and address	Full name and address
Signature Date	Signature Date

Form IHT 205: Return of Estate Information

HM Revenue & Customs

Return of estate information

Fill in this version of this form only when the person died on or after the 1st September 2006.
Fill in this form where the person who has died ("the deceased") had their permanent home in the United Kingdom at the date of death and the **gross value of the estate for inheritance tax**
- is less than the excepted estate limit, **or**   "✓" ✓
- is less than £1,000,000 **and** there is no inheritance tax to pay because of spouse, civil partner or charity exemption **only**.

About the person who has died

Title	1.1 MR	Surname	1.2 DOE
		Other name(s)	1.3 JOHN EDWARD
		Date of death	1.4 19/04/2007

Marital or civil partnership status   Write whichever is appropriate a, b, c or d in the box   1.5 **d**

a. married or in civil partnership   **b.** single   **c.** divorced or former civil partner   **d.** widowed or surviving civil partner

Occupation   1.6 RETIRED   National Insurance number   1.7 | | | | | | | |

Surviving relatives   "✓"   "✓"   "✓"

Husband/Wife or Civil Partner 1.8 | Brother(s)/Sister(s) 1.9 ✓ | Parent(s) 1.10 ✓

Number of children 1.11 2 | Number of grandchildren 1.12 5

The notes in booklet IHT206 will help you fill in this form. You must answer questions 2 - 10.

About the estate

2. Within seven years of death did the deceased

   No Yes

   a. make any gifts or other transfers totalling more than £3,000 per year, other than normal birthday, festive, marriage or civil partnership gifts, **or**   ✓ ☐

   b. give up the right to benefit from any assets held in trust that were treated as part of their estate for inheritance tax purposes (see booklet IHT206)?   ✓ ☐

   If you answer 'Yes' to either part of question 2, include the chargeable value of the gifts in box 14.1. But if this value is more than £150,000 or the assets do not qualify as 'specified transfers' (see IHT206) stop filling in this form. You will need to fill in form IHT200 instead.

3. Did the deceased make

   a. a gift, on or after 18 March 1986, where they continued to benefit from, or had some right to benefit from, or use all or part of the asset? **Or**   ✓ ☐

   b. a gift, on or after 18 March 1986, where the person receiving the gift did not take full possession of it? **Or**   ✓ ☐

   c. an election that the income tax charge should not apply to   ✓ ☐

   - assets they previously owned, in which they retained a benefit **or**

   - the deceased's contribution to the purchase price of assets acquired by another person, but in which the deceased retained a benefit?

   If you answer 'Yes' to any part of question 3, stop filling in this form. You will need to fill in form IHT200 instead.

4. Did the deceased have the right to receive the benefit from any assets held in a trust that were treated as part of their estate for inheritance tax purposes(see booklet IHT206)?   ✓ ☐

   If you answer 'Yes' to question 4 and the deceased

   - *was entitled to benefit from a single trust, and*

   - *the value of the assets in that trust, treated as part of their estate, was less than £150,000.*

   include the value of the trust assets in box 14.2. But if the value is more than £150,000, or there is more than one trust, stop filling in this form. You will need to fill in form IHT200 instead.

5. Did the deceased own or benefit from any assets outside the UK?   ✓ ☐

   If you answer 'Yes' to question 5 include the value of the overseas assets in box 14.5. But if the value of the overseas assets is more than £100,000, stop filling in this form. You will need to fill in form IHT200 instead.

IHT205 (2006)   www.hmrc.gov.uk/cto   Helpline 0845 30 20 900   HMRC 09/06

		No	Yes
6.	Did the deceased pay premiums on any life insurance policies that were not for the deceased's own benefit or did not pay out to the estate?	✓	☐
	If you answer 'Yes' to question 6, you must also answer question 11.		
7.	Did the deceased benefit from an alternatively secured pension fund (see IHT206)?	✓	☐
	*If you have answered 'Yes' to question 7 **stop filling in this form. You will need to fill in form IHT200 instead.***		
8.	Did the deceased benefit under a registered pension scheme, where		
	• the benefit was unsecured **and**		
	• they acquired the benefit as a relevant dependant of a person who died aged 75 or over?	✓	☐
	*If you have answered 'Yes' to question 8 **stop filling in this form. You will need to fill in form IHT200 instead.***		
9.	Was the deceased a member of a pension scheme or did they have a personal pension policy from which, in either case, they had not taken their full retirement benefits before the date of death?	✓	☐
	If you answer 'Yes' to question 9, you must also answer question 12.		
10. a.	Was the deceased entitled to receive payments from a pension which continued to be paid after they had died (other than arrears of pension)?	✓	☐
	b. Was a lump sum payable under a pension scheme or pension policy as a result of the death?	✓	☐
	If you answer 'Yes' to question 10, see IHT206 to find out where to include the asset.		

Do not answer questions 11 or 12 unless you answered 'Yes' to questions 6 or 9.

11. Within seven years of the death, did the deceased

   a. pay any premium on a life insurance policy under which the benefit is payable other than to the estate, or to the spouse or civil partner of the deceased, *and if so*   ☐ ☐

   b. did they buy an annuity at any time?   ☐ ☐

   *If you answer 'Yes' to question 11(a), see IHT206 to find out how to include the premiums paid on this form. If you answer 'Yes' to **both** question 11(a) & 11(b), **stop filling in this form. You will need to fill in form IHT200 instead.***

12. At a time when they were in poor health or terminally ill, did the deceased change their pension scheme or personal pension policy so as to

   a. dispose of any of the benefits payable, or   ☐ ☐

   b. make any change to the benefits to which they were entitled?   ☐ ☐

   *If you answer 'Yes' to question 12(a) or 12(b), **stop filling in this form. You will need to fill in form IHT200 instead.***

13. Deceased's own assets (including jointly owned assets NOT passing by survivorship - see IHT206)

   • *You must include the gross value for each item below, before deduction of any exemption or relief.*

   • *You must include all the assets that were part of the deceased's estate as at the date of death, ignoring any changes that may take place through an Instrument of Variation made after the death.*

   • *You must make full enquiries so that you can show that the figures that you give in this form are right. If you cannot find out the value for an item, you may include your best estimate.*

Tick box to show estimated amounts '✓'

13.1	Cash, including money in banks, building societies and National Savings	13.1	£13,850	☐
13.2	Household and personal goods	13.2		☐
13.3	Stocks and shares quoted on the Stock Exchange	13.3		☐
13.4	Stocks and shares not quoted on the Stock Exchange	13.4		☐
13.5	Insurance policies, including bonuses and mortgage protection policies	13.5	£5,000	✓
13.6	Money owed to the person who has died	13.6		☐
13.7	Partnership and business interests	13.7		☐
13.8	Freehold/leasehold residence of the person who has died	13.8	£250,000	✓

Address *(including postcode)*
27 THE DRIVE, HOMETOWN, ANYSHIRE HT27 5ZA

www.hmrc.gov.uk/cto   *Helpline 0845 30 20 900*

Tick box to show estimated amounts "✓"

13.9 Other freehold/leasehold residential property — **13.9**
Address (including postcode)

13.10 Other land and buildings — **13.10**
Address/location

13.11 Any other assets not included above — **13.11**

Total estate for which a grant is required (sum of boxes 13.1 to 13.11) **A** £268,850

14. Other assets forming part of the estate

14.1 Gifts and other lifetime transfers (after deduction of exemptions) — **14.1**
Details of gifts

14.2 Assets held in trust for the benefit of the deceased — **14.2**
Details of assets held in trust

14.3 Share of joint assets passing automatically to the surviving joint owner — **14.3**
Details of joint assets

14.4 Nominated assets — **14.4**

14.5 Assets outside the United Kingdom (value in £ sterling) — **14.5**

Total (sum of boxes 14.1 to 14.5) **B** £0

Gross estate for inheritance tax (A + B) **C** £268,850

15. Debts of the estate

15.1 Funeral expenses — **15.1** £3,756

15.2 Mortgage or share of a mortgage on a property in Section 13 — **15.2**

15.3 Other debts owed by the deceased in the UK — **15.3** £1,330

Total debts owing in the UK (sum of boxes 15.1 to 15.3) **D** £5,086

15.4 Debts payable out of trust assets — **15.4**

15.5 Share of mortgage on a property owned as a joint asset — **15.5**

15.6 Share of other debts payable out of joint assets — **15.6**

15.7 Debts owing to persons outside the UK — **15.7**

Total of other debts (sum of boxes 15.4 to 15.7) **E** £0

Total debts (D + E) **F** £5,086

Net estate for inheritance tax (C - F) **G** £263,764

16. | Use this space to provide any other information we have asked for or you would like taken into account.

17. **Exemptions (you should read IHT206 before filling in this section)**

In the box below, deduct any exemption for assets passing on death to
* the spouse or civil partner of the deceased, or

* a UK charity or for national purposes

Describe the extent of the exemption deducted. If for charities, etc give the name of the charity(s) or other organisation(s) benefiting. Where exemptions are deducted for particular assets, list those assets and show the amount deducted.

17.1

	H	£0	
Net qualifying value for excepted estates (G - H)	J	£263,764	

17.2 Tax district and/or income tax reference number | 17.2

If the value in box J is more than the excepted estate limit, you must fill in form IHT200.

If you find something has been left out, or if any of the figures you have given in this form change later on, you only need to tell us if, taking all the omissions and changes into account,
* the figure at box G is now higher than the inheritance tax threshold, **and**
* there are no exemptions to deduct which keep the value at box J below the inheritance tax threshold.

If, at any time, the value at box J is more than the inheritance tax threshold, you must list any new items and the items that have changed in a Corrective Account (form C4) and send it to us with a copy of this form along with a cheque for the tax that has become payable.

The issue of the grant does not mean that there is no inheritance tax due on this estate.

To the best of my/our knowledge and belief, the information I/we have given in this form is correct and complete. I/We have read and understand the statements above.

I/We understand that I/we may have to pay financial penalties if the answers to the questions or figures that I/we give in this form are wrong because of my/our negligence or fraud, OR if the estate fails to qualify as an excepted estate and I/we do not deliver a corrective account within 6 months of the failure coming to my/our notice.

Full name and address	Full name and address
PAUL MICHAEL DOE 4 THE CRESCENT ANYTOWN LOAMSHIRE A21 2XY	JENNIFER ALICE DOE 4 THE CRESCENT ANYTOWN LOAMSHIRE A21 2XY
Signature *P Doe* Date 10/12/2007	Signature *J Doe* Date 10/12/2007
Full name and address	Full name and address
Signature Date	Signature Date

Summary

Gross estate in the United Kingdom passing under Will or by intestacy		A	£268,850
Debts in the United Kingdom owed by the deceased alone		D	£5,086
Net estate in the United Kingdom	(A - D)	K	£263,764

www.hmrc.gov.uk/cto   *Helpline 0845 30 20 900*

Form D1: The Will

HM Revenue & Customs

The Will

Name

JOHN EDWARD DOE

Date of death

19 / 04 / 2007

Give details and provide a copy of the latest Will made by the deceased, together with any codicils. If a Deed of Variation has been signed before applying for a grant, fill in the form to show the effect of the Will and the Deed together. You should read form D1(Notes) before filling in this form.

1 Is the address for the deceased as shown in the Will the same as the address on page 1 of form IHT200?

No ☐   Yes ✓

If the answer is "No", say below what happened to the property shown in the Will.

2 Are all items referred to in the Will, for example, legacies referring to personal possessions, stocks and shares, loans or gifts made by the deceased, included in form IHT200?

N/A ☐   No ☐   Yes ✓

If the answer is "No", say below why these items are not included.

3 Does the whole estate pass to beneficiaries who are chargeable to inheritance tax?

No ☐   Yes ✓

If the answer is "No", deduct the exemption on form IHT200.

D1   www.hmrc.gov.uk/cto   Helpline 0845 30 20 900   HMRC CT 08/06

Form D4: Joint and Nominated Assets

2 **Land, buildings, business assets, control shareholdings and unquoted shares**

Do you wish to pay tax on these assets by instalments?　　　　　　No ☐　Yes ☐

If the value of the deceased's share is **not** the **whole** value, say

- who the other joint owner(s) is or are
- when the joint ownership began
- how much each joint owner provided to obtain the item
- who received the income, if there was any
- whether the item passes to other joint owner(s) by survivorship or under the deceased's Will or intestacy.

NONE

Details of each item	Whole value	Deceased's share
NONE		

	Total of assets	JP6	£0

- Liabilities

	Total of liabilities	JP7	£0

	Net assets *(box JP6 less box JP7)*	JP8	£0

- Exemptions and reliefs

	Total exemptions and reliefs	JP9	£0

Net total of joint assets *passing by survivorship* where tax may be paid by instalments *(box JP8 less box JP9)*	JP10	£0

3 **Nominated property**

If the deceased nominated any assets to any person, describe the assets below and show their value.

NONE

Include the assets in the appropriate box in section F of form IHT200.

Form D10: Household and Personal Goods

HM Revenue & Customs — Household and personal goods

Name
JOHN EDWARD DOE

Date of death
19/04/2007

Give details about the household goods or other personal property owned by the deceased. You should read form D10(Notes) before filling in this form. You should forward any professional valuations obtained.

HG1 Did the deceased own any of the following

	Yes	No
Motor vehicles including vintage and classic vehicles	✓	
Motor cycles		✓
Caravans		✓
Aeroplanes		✓
Boats		✓
Other		✓

If you have answered yes to any of the above, go to question HG2 otherwise go to question HG5

HG2 Provide the following information in respect of each item that has not been sold.

Manufacturer	Model	Year of manufacture or first registration	Registration number (where appropriate)	Condition	Value
TOYOTA	PRIUS	2005	NG497XY	GOOD	£12,000
			Vehicles etc. that have not been sold Total HG2		£12,000

HG3 Provide the following information in respect of each item that has been sold.

Manufacturer	Model	Year of manufacture or first registration	Registration number (where appropriate)	Condition	Date of sale	Sale price or value at date of death
LAND ROVER	DEFENDER	1999	YU432AB	GOOD	01/06/07	£7,000
			Vehicles etc. that have been sold Total HG2			£7,000

HG4 What was the relationship between the purchaser and the deceased?

Item	Relationship
	NONE

D10   www.hmrc.gov.uk/cto   Helpline 0845 30 20 900   HMRC CT 08/06

		Yes	No
HG5	Did the deceased own any jewellery? *If you have answered yes to this question, go to question HG6 otherwise go to question HG9.*	✓	

HG6 Provide the following information about the jewellery that has not been sold.

Item	Description	Value
MISCELLANEOUS RINGS, BROOCHES, ETC	MODERN (MID 20TH CENTURY). INHERITED FROM WIFE.	£1,500
	Jewellery that has not been sold Total HG6	£1,500

HG7 Provide the following information about the jewellery that has been sold.

Item	Description	Date of sale	Sale price or value at date of death
	NONE		
	Jewellery that has been sold Total HG7		£0

HG8 What was the relationship between the purchaser and the deceased?

Item	Relationship
	NONE

		Yes	No
HG9	Did the deceased own any	✓	

- antiques or works of art including paintings, drawings, sculpture porcelain, glass, silver etc.? or
- collections of any kind such as books, stamps, coins, medals or wines and spirits

If you have answered yes to this question go to question HG10 otherwise go to question HG13.

HG10 Give full details of the items that have not been sold.

Item	Description	Value
TWO 19TH CENTURY WATER COLOURS	MINOR ARTISTS	£1,500
	Antiques etc. that have not been sold Total HG10	£1,500

HG11 Give full details of the items that have been sold.

Item	Description	Date of sale	Sale price or value at date of death
	NONE		

Antiques etc. that have been sold Total HG11	£0

HG12 What was the relationship between the purchaser and the deceased?

Item	Relationship
	NONE

HG13 Give details of all other household and personal goods that have not been sold. Include all televisions, audio video equipment, cameras and other specialist equipment, electrical equipment, furniture, household and domestic items, clothes, garden equipment, tools etc.

Item	Description	Value
	NONE	

Other household and personal goods that have not been sold Total HG13	£0

HG14 Give details of all other household and personal goods that have been sold. Include all televisions, audio video equipment, cameras and other specialist equipment, electrical equipment, furniture, household and domestic items, clothes, garden equipment, tools etc.

Item	Description	Date of sale	Sale price or value at date of death

Other household and personal goods that have been sold Total HG14	£0

HG15 What was the relationship between the purchaser and the deceased?

Item	Relationship

HG16 If you have not obtained professional valuations please say how you valued the household and personal effects. If the household and personal effects are considered to be valueless please explain why. If the deceased did not own any household goods or personal possessions explain the circumstances here.

THE VALUATIONS OF ITEMS HG6 AND HG10 WERE INFORMAL AND BASED ON DICUSSIONS WITH LOCAL SHOPKEEPERS.
THE REST OF THE HOUSEHOLD GOODS ARE STANDARD ITEMS (TV, RADIO, CARPETS ETC.) AND ARE OF NO SALEABLE VALUE.

HG17 Bring the totals of the items that have not been sold forward and add them up.

Total HG2	£12,000
Total HG6	£1,500
Total HG10	£1,500
Total HG13	£0
Overall total for the unsold personal goods. Copy to box F20 on form IHT200	£15,000

HG18 Bring the totals of the items that have been sold forward and add them up.

Total HG3	£7,000
Total HG7	£0
Total HG11	£0
Total HG 14	£0
Overall value of the personal goods that have been sold. Copy to box F19 on form IHT200	£7,000

The values to be included are those before exemptions. Exemptions should be shown on the IHT200.

Form D12: Land, Buildings and Interests in Land

HM Revenue & Customs

Land, buildings and interests in land

Name

JOHN EDWARD DOE

Date of death

19/04/2007

CT reference

Give the details we ask for about the land included in the deceased's estate. You should read form D12(Notes) before filling in this form.

Name and address of the person that the Valuation Office should contact

Reference

PAUL MICHAEL DOE
4 THE CRESCENT
ANYTOWN
LOAMSHIRE AZ1 2XY

Telephone number

01573 859000

A Item No.	B Full address or description of property	Post Code	C Tenure	D Lettings/leases	E Agricultural, timber or heritage element	F Open market value
1	27 THE DRIVE, HOMETOWN, ANYSHIRE	HT27 5ZA	FREEHOLD	N/A	N/A	£750,000
				Total(s) carried forward	£0	£750,000

www.hmrc.gov.uk/cto   Helpline 0845 30 20 900

Please turn over
HMRC CT1205

D12

108

A Item No.	B Full address or description of property	Post Code	C Tenure	D Lettings/leases	E Agricultural, timber or heritage element	F Open market value
	Total(s) brought forward				£0	£750,000
				Total(s)	£0	£750,000

3 Were any of the properties subject to any damage that may affect their value?   No ☐   Yes ☐

If the answer is "Yes", fill in the box below using the same item number(s) that you have used in column A above.

Item No.	Details of damage

4 Have any of the properties been sold, or do you intend to sell any of them within 12 months?   No ☐   Yes ☑

If the answer is "Yes", fill in table below using the same item number(s) that you have used in column A above.

G Item No.	H Present position of sale	I Sale price	J Type of sale	K Price for fixtures, carpets and curtains	L Use sale price as value
1	WILL BE SOLD WHEN PROBATE GRANTED. NOT YET ON THE MARKET.				

Form D18: Probate Summary

Inland Revenue
Capital Taxes

Probate summary

Fill in this page to give details of the estate that becomes the property of the personal representatives of the deceased. It is this property for which the grant of representation is to be made. You should read form D18(Notes) before filling in this form.

A Name and address

Probate registry

Principal

Date of grant
(for probate registry use)

B About the person who has died

Title: MR

Surname: DOE

First name(s): JOHN EDWARD

Date of death: 19/04/2007

Domicile: ENGLAND & WALES

Last known usual address

27 THE DRIVE
HOMETOWN
ANYSHIRE

Postcode HT27 5ZA

C Summary from IHT200
Add the value of any general power property on form D5 to boxes PS1-PS5

Gross assets, section F, box 24	PS1	£92,268
Gross assets, section G, box 13	PS2	£750,000
Gross value to be carried to Probate papers *(box PS1 plus box PS2)*	PS3	£842,268
Liabilities, section F, box F27	PS4	£3,348
Liabilities, section G, boxes G14 plus G15	PS5	£0
Net value to be carried to Probate papers *(box PS3 less box PS4 less box PS5)*	PS6	£838,920
Tax and interest paid on this account, section J, box J19	PS7	£0.00

P Doe
Signature of person or firm calculating the amount due

Paul Michael Doe
Contact name and /or reference

10 / 12 / 2007
Date

(For IR CT use only)

IR CT reference

EDP

Cashier's reference

IR CT Cashiers

D18 (PDF) Version 2.0.0.2

R0G4109CTO11/99

Chapter 6

Obtaining the Grant

Sending in the Application

When you have completed the forms you are ready to make the application. You have chosen the most convenient registry and all that remains is to send the forms there. We have suggested that you post your application rather than take it in person but, if you wish, you may take the forms into the registry or sub-registry. You should not take your forms to a probate office, as it may not be open.

All the application forms described in Chapter 5 which you have completed, together with the death certificate, and the original will along with any codicils, should be sent in. If you are using the post, special delivery is obviously safest. For your own reference, it is a good idea to take photocopies of all the documents before sending them. You should send the original death certificate issued by the registrar (not a photocopy) and the original will. Although the death certificate will be returned to you, the will and codicil remain with the court. The fee should be sent in as well. Full details of the fees payable are set out in the documents which accompanied the forms, and they are very simple. The fee is calculated on the net amount of the estate, that is the value of the estate less the debts and funeral expenses. If this is £5,000 or less, there is no fee. If the value exceeds £5,000, the fee is £90.00. In addition, if you want any copies of the grant (which will be useful if you have a number of separate assets to collect), they are £1.00 each. It is as well to get them now as the price goes up to £5.00 if you order them after the grant issues. The cheque should be made payable to "HM Courts Service" (or "HMCS"). Unfortunately, there are no facilities outside the Principal Registry in London to accept debit or credit cards and you are strongly advised not to send cash with your application. If you do not have a bank account, the fees can be paid by postal order.

It is possible to have the fees remitted, either partially or in total. For example, if you are in receipt of income support you may be entitled to a full remission. If you wish to look into this further, you should contact the registry where you will be making the application and ask for form EX160. Having read this, if you think you qualify, you should complete and return it to the registry, preferably with your application forms. You should send in any documents in support of your application (such as letters confirming the amount and type of benefit you receive). Your application will be considered and the question of the fee resolved before the grant issues. In fact, the grant cannot issue until the fee is either paid or remitted.

The original will is the document which is to be "proved" and it must be examined by the registry. On pages 23–24 the dangers of altering a will were mentioned, as were the difficulties which may arise if anything is attached to the will. As marks may not be visible on a copy, it is essential the original will is lodged, so that any question raised by pin or staple marks, or any alterations, can be resolved as quickly as possible. This applies equally to any codicil.

As soon as the application is received at the registry, a process is set in motion which will result in the issue of a grant. Usually, an application is processed on the day it is received but, on occasions, and at certain times of the year, so many are sent in that arrears build up and there may be a short delay. In any event, you should hear from the registry within two weeks of sending in your forms.

The papers are checked in the registry to make sure that they have been completed correctly and that you are entitled to make the application. The person who examines your papers makes a note of any queries which arise.

The registry then writes to you if necessary, fixing an appointment for you to attend at the venue of your choice to complete the formalities. In most registries it is the practice to telephone the applicant with any enquiries regarding the papers before the interview.

Generally, appointments are fixed on a "next turn" basis, but if you have any preferences, or if there are any days when you cannot attend, please make a note on your PA1 form or in a covering letter. The same applies to any times during the day which are not convenient for you. The registries are open during office hours only, so evening or weekend appointments are not possible. It is likely that you will have to wait longer for an appointment at a probate office than at the main registry or sub-registry.

Your letter from the registry gives the date, time and place of your appointment. Occasionally, time becomes available at short notice and the registry may telephone to ask if you would like to accept an early appointment. Normally, you will have plenty of time before the appointment to make arrangements for someone to accompany you if you wish. There will also be a map on the back of the letter showing the location of the office you have chosen. Although it is a rare occurrence, occasionally appointment letters are mixed up and you may find yourself being given an appointment at an office you have not chosen. This would always be a mistake and you should contact the registry or sub-registry which sent out the appointment and have matters corrected.

It is important to read the appointment letter carefully to find out whether you need to bring any documents with you, and to check the place, date and time of the interview. You will be asked to bring along two proofs of identity. These are set out in form PA6 mentioned in the previous chapter, but basically they are:

- a full driving licence;
- your passport;
- your official bus pass;
- your national insurance or national health card;
- your state pension or child benefit notification letter;
- a utilities bill showing your current address;
- your council tax bill.

The letter from the registry is also a receipt for the death certificate and will (if any). It may ask you to bring either or both of these documents if you did not send them in with your papers (although you are more likely to be asked for the original will before you get an appointment letter if you have not sent it in with your application). There may be other documents attached, for example requests for witnesses to attend if there is some doubt about the execution of the will or renunciation, or power of attorney forms which need to be completed (see page 48). The letter will set out what forms are attached and give instructions about completing and returning them. Please be sure to read all the instructions carefully, as the speed with which your grant issues is likely to depend on how quickly you return the forms, properly completed.

Paying Inheritance Tax

If it was necessary to complete Form IHT200, you should have lodged the completed Form D18 with your application papers. This will be returned to you with your appointment letter; the name and address of the registry where you are making your application will have been added. You should send form D18 to HM Revenue and Customs at the address shown on the form, together with your completed form IHT200 and any of the relevant supplementary pages. HM Revenue and Customs then completes form D18 and returns it to the registry where you have made your application. This may be a matter of simply stamping the form if there is no inheritance tax to pay, or it may require that any tax due is paid before the form can be returned.

If there is no inheritance tax to pay, HM Revenue and Customs endorses Form D18 and returns it to the probate registry. The grant is then issued. If inheritance tax is payable, HM Revenue and Customs calculates the amount and notifies you. The payment should be sent directly to them and they then stamp the D18 to prove that the tax has been paid and return it to the probate registry where the grant can then be issued.

It is possible for you to calculate the amount of inheritance tax yourself and plenty of guidance is available in booklet IHT213 mentioned in the Chapter 5. If you are confident you can do so (or are sure that no tax is payable), you can complete the assessment and send a cheque to cover the inheritance tax (or the part immediately payable) when you send the forms to HM Revenue and Customs. The procedure in sending in the forms is the same.

The registry is obliged by the Supreme Court Act 1981 to ensure that all tax immediately due is paid before it can issue the grant. The procedure is relatively straightforward, although paying the tax may not be so.

As the assets constituting the estate are frozen from the date of the deceased's death they cannot, except in some special circumstances, be used to pay the tax.

Often there is insufficient ready cash in the estate to pay inheritance tax which is due immediately, but there are many ways of raising the money. For example, you may be able to use money held in the deceased's bank or building society account to pay inheritance tax, and the procedure is set out in explanatory booklet SP2 which is part of the HM Revenue and Customs forms package (see Chapter 5). This should be read carefully and the instructions followed. If the deceased had money in savings certificates or in premium bonds, the cash can be used to pay all or part of the tax due. Further information about inheritance tax, and any other aspects of it, can be obtained by telephoning the Probate and Inheritance Tax helpline on 0845 302 0900. You should bear in mind that paying tax by this method may be a lengthy process. and may cause unacceptable delay.

It may be necessary to borrow from a bank to finance the payment of tax. The bank should be asked to provide a loan account specifically for this purpose. The loan will obviously attract interest, but the interest charges may be offset against any liability for income tax the estate may incur.

If you are the only beneficiary of the estate, or one of the main beneficiaries, it is worth considering paying the tax from your own, or from other beneficiaries', resources. This is especially attractive when the interest on a loan would be high – the cost of borrowing reduces the residue of the estate left for the beneficiaries. If you are not a beneficiary yourself, those who are beneficiaries may choose this course rather than borrowing to pay the tax.

Going to Court

The time is now approaching when you will attend your interview. Although the probate registries are courts of law, your interview is conducted in private and is quite informal. You will be treated with sympathy and tact and the process should be efficient and take no longer than necessary (usually, fifteen minutes is allowed for each interview). The procedure differs from office to office and from registry to registry but there are certain points which are common to all.

On arrival, if you are attending a main or sub-registry, there will be someone to report to in the reception room. At a probate office, the attending officer may ask you to produce your appointment letter, which will help the officer locate the papers.

Either before or during the interview, you will be given certain documents which have been prepared in the registry from the information in the forms you completed earlier. You will be given a document called an "oath". This is, in fact, a single page affidavit which contains details of the deceased, the applicant, the value of the estate and the entitlement of the applicant to have the grant. It also contains a statement that you will administer the deceased's estate according to the law. This document must be "sworn" (or "affirmed"), and you should read it carefully. Although prepared by the probate registry, you are responsible for the accuracy of the facts set out in the oath.

If you do not understand anything in the forms or documents you are given, ask the officer who interviews you to explain. Remember, you will be swearing to the accuracy of the statements in the oath and it is important that you do not do so until you are completely satisfied that you understand the contents fully. If you find any any mistakes in the forms, please point them out. Usually they are accurate, but errors do occur and if not spotted at the time of swearing, you may have to pay a second visit to the office.

There may be some questions to be dealt with. Perhaps the figures require clarification, or there may be some point on the names which requires attention. Once these have been resolved, the officer can complete the papers and you will be asked to sign the oath and the other documents which are required. This is usually the stage where you will be asked to produce your proofs of identity. All the documents, once read, will be returned to you.

You should sign with your usual signature, whether that be initial and surname or your full name. The officer (also known as the "commissioner") will then ask you to swear to the truth of the oath and the other affidavits (if there are any). Each registry should have religious books for the faiths of all applicants. If you have no religious faith or your faith precludes you from taking an oath, you should tell the officer, who will make the necessary amendments to the papers so that you may instead "affirm" the truth of the documents. The oath and the affirmation are equally binding.

Assuming you wish to swear the papers, the commissioner will ask you to stand (unless you are unable to do so), to take the testament in your right hand and read the words of the oath from the card given to you, or to repeat the words after the commissioner. This is the point in the proceedings which is the most emotional and it is not at all unusual for applicants (both men and women) to break down. If this happens to you, there is no need to be embarrassed. You are not the first person to do so and will certainly not be the last. Unfortunately, the words of the oath or the affirmation have to be said, no matter how upsetting, and so you will be required to speak them, in full, even if it means another start. This is the most formal part of the application, and the grant of probate or letters of administration is based on the contents of the documents which you swear or affirm.

Usually, you need attend the registry only once, to swear or affirm the papers, but, as was said previously, some registries arrange preliminary appointments if there is a problem which prevents the registry from proceeding. In such a case, the appointment letter will make it clear that two visits will be necessary. This type of arrangement is fairly unusual; queries are sometimes dealt with by telephone or by correspondence, but some applications are so complicated that an interview is necessary to clarify preliminary points.

The Issue of the Grant

There remains the most important matter – the issue of the grant. Unless you wish to make arrangements to collect it from the registry, the grant is sent by post following the interview. There are few hold-ups once the papers have been sworn. If inheritance tax is payable, this adds to the time taken for the grant to issue – at the very least, HM Revenue and Customs have to receive your payment of tax and issue a receipt. It is possible that witness evidence may be required to establish the validity of the will; although there is no harm in swearing the papers before that evidence is obtained, the grant cannot issue until the witnesses have given evidence and the will is demonstrated to be capable of proof. These two examples of delay after swearing the application papers are not particularly common and usually the grant can be issued within ten working days of the formalities being completed and the fee paid, although sometimes it may take a little longer.

Finally, the envelope containing the grant is delivered. The "letters of administration" document (the grant issued if there was no will) is always one sheet. A "grant of probate" (where there was a will) and a grant of "letters of administration (with will)" (where there was a will but no executors were appointed or the appointment of executors has failed) are both bound together with a copy of the will and any codicils attached. Examples are set out on the pages which follow.

In all cases, the grant shows the name, address, date of death and domicile of the deceased, and your (and your co-executors' or administrators', if any) names and addresses. It also shows the gross and net estate, either as a sum which the estate does not exceed or the actual figures, depending upon the circumstances. It is sealed with the seal of the High Court, dated, and signed either by a district probate registrar or a probate officer.

Always check the grant to ensure that the details set out are accurate and that you have the correct number of copies. Any doubts or errors should be reported at once to the registry which issued the grant, to enable any mistake to be rectified.

At last, you have the grant and you are ready to start administering the estate. The next chapter explains how to do this.

Example Grant of Probate

COPIES OF THIS GRANT ARE NOT VALID UNLESS
THEY BEAR THE IMPRESSED SEAL OF THE COURT

IN THE HIGH COURT OF JUSTICE
The District Probate Registry at Winchester

BE IT KNOWN that John Edward Doe otherwise Jack Doe
of 1, The Avenue, Anytown, Loamshire LO17 9QQ

died on the 23rd day of February 2007
domiciled in England and Wales

AND BE IT FURTHER KNOWN that the last Will and Testament of the
said deceased (a copy of which is annexed) was proved and registered in
the High Court of Justice and that Administration of all the estate which
by law devolves to and vests in the personal representative of the said
deceased was granted by the High Court of Justice on this date to the
Executor

RICHARD FRANCIS DOE of 1 The Avenue, Anytown,
Loamshire LO17 9QQ

Power reserved to another executor

It is hereby certified that it appears from information supplied on the
application for this grant that the gross value of the said estate in the
United Kingdom does not exceed £300,000 and the net value of such
estate does not exceed £25,000.

Dated the 8th day of May 2007

(Signature)

District Registrar/Probate Officer

Extracted personally

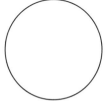

PROBATE

Example Grant of Letters of Administration (With Will Annexed)

COPIES OF THIS GRANT ARE NOT VALID UNLESS THEY BEAR THE IMPRESSED SEAL OF THE COURT

IN THE HIGH COURT OF JUSTICE
The District Probate Registry at Winchester

BE IT KNOWN that CHARLES DOE
of 1, The Avenue, Anytown, Loamshire LO17 9QQ

died on the 29th day of April 2007
domiciled in England and Wales

AND BE IT FURTHER KNOWN that the last Will and Testament of the said deceased (a copy of which is annexed) was proved and registered in the High Court of Justice and that Administration of all the estate which by law devolves to and vests in the personal representative of the said deceased was granted by the High Court of Justice on this date to

MARY DOE of 1 The Avenue, Anytown, Loamshire LO17 9QQ

It is hereby certified that it appears from information supplied on the application for this grant that the gross value of the said estate in the United Kingdom does not exceed £300,000 and the net value of such estate does not exceed £25,000.

Dated the 8th day of May 2008

(Signature)

District Registrar/Probate Officer

Extracted personally

ADMIN/WILL

Example Grant of Letters of Administration

COPIES OF THIS GRANT ARE NOT VALID UNLESS
THEY BEAR THE IMPRESSED SEAL OF THE COURT

IN THE HIGH COURT OF JUSTICE
The District Probate Registry at Winchester

BE IT KNOWN that `Mary Doe`
of `1, The Avenue, Anytown, Loamshire LO17 9QQ`

died on the `4th day of May 2007`
domiciled in `England and Wales INTESTATE`

AND BE IT FURTHER KNOWN that Administration of all the estate
which by law devolves to and vests in the personal representative of the
said deceased was granted by the High Court of Justice on this date to

`ROBIN DOE of 1 The Avenue, Anytown, Loamshire LO17
9QQ`

It is hereby certified that it appears from information supplied on the
application for this grant that the gross value of the said estate in the
United Kingdom does not exceed £300,000 and the net value of such
estate does not exceed £25,000.

Dated the `5th day of July 2007`

Signature)

District Registrar/Probate Officer

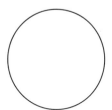

Extracted personally

ADMINISTRATION

Chapter 7

Collecting the Estate

Armed with the authority of the grant of probate or administration, you can now proceed to collect together all the goods and other property in the estate. Items which are to be sold can now be sold and the proceeds paid into the estate bank account. Any income received by the estate, or debts incurred by it, since the date of death must be taken into account; careful records must be kept. It is crucial you do not "mix" any of your own money with the estate or pay any estate money into your own account. At the end of this process, the balance left in the estate can be given to those who are entitled to receive it.

This procedure of collecting together the assets and debts of the estate, and then paying them out (or "distributing" them), is called "administering the estate". This chapter deals with collecting the estate together; Chapter 8 deals with paying it out.

As before, this chapter is written as though there is only one personal representative dealing with the estate; if there are more, they take joint responsibility.

Personal Representatives' Responsibility

The personal representative – the executor or administrator to whom the grant has been issued – has certain responsibilities. We have already seen (page 116) that when swearing the oath, the personal representative gives an undertaking (promise) to the court to deal with the estate according to the legal requirements. As we will see below, he or she must make sure that the value of the estate is kept as high as possible. When selling anything which forms part of the estate to friends or relatives, care must be taken to ensure that sales are conducted at arm's length so the best possible price is obtained.

Generally, the personal representative is responsible for completing any outstanding legal obligation of the deceased person, for example, the personal representative must complete the sale or purchase of property if contracts had been exchanged by the deceased. But there are some obligations which cease on death and do not fall to the personal representative. These include any obligation to pay maintenance to a former spouse or civil partner, or to children. A former spouse, civil partner or a child may of course bring an inheritance a claim under the Inheritance etc Act (see page 132). The personal representative can be sued for a debt or other matter for which the deceased could have been sued.

This may sound daunting, but these duties are on the personal representative in his or her capacity as personal representative of the deceased – not in a personal capacity. Further, the liability of the personal representative for debts cannot exceed the value of the assets in the estate.

The Assets

All the items which constitute the estate should have been declared in Form IHT205 or Form IHT200. If tax is due, the grant cannot issue until the tax has been paid. The court has a statutory duty to ensure that all tax due is paid, or that no tax is payable, before it issues the grant. Once the grant of probate or administration has been issued, it is time to use it to collect together all these assets.

Each asset-holder – bank, building society or other organisation – needs to see either the original grant, or a copy bearing the court seal. You will have asked for copies at the probate registry (see page 111) and you should have received them with the grant. If you need further copies they can be obtained from the issuing registry on payment of the relevant fees.

We have already suggested (see page 60) that you open an account in your name as the personal representative of the deceased. If you have not already opened an account, now is the time to do so and, as was previously suggested, it is often more convenient to open this account at the bank or building society where the deceased's account is held. Into this account you should pay all money received during the process of collecting in the assets, keeping a record of the amounts and who paid them. These details will be needed later to complete the estate account (see page 137).

We next look at how to deal with the specific items which make up the estate.

Personal Chattels

A personal representative is under a duty to maximise the value of the estate, so that the residuary beneficiary or beneficiaries (who may indeed include the personal representative) receive all that is due. When assets are to be sold, the best price must therefore be obtained. On page 55, the meaning of "personal chattels" was explained. These goods must be sold unless they are specifically given to someone by a will or they pass under the intestacy rules (see page 139). The proceeds of sale should be paid into the personal representative's bank account for the estate until the time comes to distribute the money to those entitled.

The goods should be sold at auction rather than privately, since sale by auction is considered to fetch the best price and can give rise to no criticism from beneficiaries that the best price was not obtained. Sale by private treaty is acceptable, provided the price obtained reflects the value and those interested in the residue agree the value. Internet auctions, including sales through e-bay, are permitted, but again the proviso that the personal representatives must obtain the best possible price applies. It is for you as personal representative to decide the best way to dispose of assets which must be sold and to achieve the sale by the most economic method.

It is difficult to sell clothes as the value is often small. The personal representative may feel it appropriate to donate the clothes to charity, but before doing so, he or she should obtain the consent of those entitled to the residue of the estate. It is also advisable to make a careful check for anything of value in the pockets, or any jewellery attached. The residuary beneficiaries are the persons prejudiced by any sale below proper market value.

Special care should be taken with organisations which advertise "house clearances". They do provide a useful service, but do not necessarily give the best price. Individual items may fetch more if sold separately. This is a matter for you as the personal representative. You can always arrange to have an expert valuation of things such as paintings, jewellery, furniture and antiques, and send them to auction if appropriate. Indeed, if there is any possibility the deceased owned any item of especial value, it is incumbent on you to have that item valued and sold at an appropriate auction. However, there is no problem with a sale by private treaty if sold after proper valuation. There can be no criticism of a sale negotiated at arm's length on the basis of proper professional advice.

Stocks and Shares

If the deceased's shareholdings are large, or are in a variety of companies, it may be advisable to instruct a stock broker or bank to deal with them. Under the Trustee Act 2000 any personal representative may use a professional to assist in the administration of the estate where to do so is in the estate's best interests. This is likely to be appropriate where shares are to be sold, since a buyer or buyers must be found. It may also be suitable if the shares are to be transferred to a number of beneficiaries.

Most banks handle share transactions and it may be convenient to use the bank the deceased used, or the bank where the account of the estate is. If the deceased had a stock broker, you may want to ask that firm to handle the shares.

Brokers and banks have different scales of charges and it is wise to ask for more than one estimate of the cost of handling the transactions.

The bank or stock broker selected will need complete instructions in writing about what is to be done with the shares.

It may appear daunting to handle the sale of shares yourself, but do not be put off. You will have to obtain forms of transfer/sale. The instructions from the company's share registrar are clear and easily understood. Illustrations of completed forms are set out on pages 127–128. Blank forms can be bought from a law stationer. To transfer shares from one person to another, a properly completed form of transfer, together with a copy of the grant of representation and the appropriate share certificate, should be sent to the registrar of the company concerned.

If the shares are to be transferred to more than one person, a separate form for each transferee should be completed.

The form includes a certificate which should be completed since stamp duty is not payable. The certificate is as follows:

"I certify that this instrument falls within category . . . of the schedule to the Stamp Duty (Exempt Instruments) Regulations 1987."

The categories are "B" where the transfer is under a specific legacy in the will; "E" where the transfer is part of the distribution of the residuary estate; and "C" where the transfer is part of the distribution of the estate under an intestacy.

The company registrar will accept the authority of the grant of representation as sufficient to enable the personal representative named in it to transfer the shares to the beneficiaries.

Where the personal representative is himself or herself the beneficiary, he or she may transfer the shares by lodging a "letter of request" (see page 129). Again, the form can be obtained from a law stationer if it not supplied by the company registrar. The best advice we can give is to write to the company registrar for the appropriate forms; in this way you can be sure to have what is required for what needs to be done.

In due course the registrar will issue new share certificates to the beneficiaries as evidence of their ownership.

The estate may be liable to pay capital gains tax on any increase in the capital value of shares between the date of death and the date they are sold or transferred to the beneficiaries. This is dealt with on page 134.

Stock Transfer Form

CON 40 (1963)

STOCK TRANSFER FORM	(Above this line for Registrars only)

Certificate lodged with the Registrar

Consideration Money: £ 30,000   (For completion by the Registrar/Stock Exchange)

Name of Undertaking.	KRADDOCK SECURITIES
Description of Security.	30,000 x £1 ORDINARY SHARES

Number or amount of Shares, Stock or other security and, in figures column only, number and denomination of units, if any.	Words THIRTY THOUSAND	Figures 30,000
		(units of £1)

Name(s) of registered holder(s) should be given in full; the address should be given where there is only one holder. If the transfer is not made by the registered holder(s) insert also the name(s) and capacity (eg, executor(s)) of the person(s) making the transfer.	PAUL MICHAEL DOE 4 THE CRESCENT ANYTOWN LOAMSHIRE A21 2XY EXECUTOR OF JOHN EDWARD DOE, DECEASED

I/We hereby transfer the above security out of the name(s) aforesaid to the person(s) named below.

Stamp of Selling Broker(s) or, for transactions which are not Stock Exchange transactions, of Agent(s), if any, acting for the Transferor(s).

Signature(s) of transferor(s)

1. _D Doe_
2. ....
3. ....
4. ....

A body corporate should execute this transfer under its common seal or otherwise in accordance with applicable statutory requirements.

Date ....

Full name(s), full postal address(es) (including county or, if applicable, postal district number) of the person(s) to whom the security is transferred. Please state title, if any, or whether Mr, Mrs or Miss Please complete in typewriting or in BLOCK CAPITALS.	MISS JESSICA EMILY DOE 3 THE CRESCENT ANYTOWN ANYSHIRE AN6 4GH

I/We request that such entries be made in the register as are necessary to give effect to this transfer.

Stamp of Buying Broker(s) if any	Stamp or name and address of person lodging this form if other than the Buying Broker(s)

Reference to the Registrar in this form means the registrar or registration agent of the undertaking NOT the Registrar of Companies at Companies House.

FORM OF CERTIFICATE REQUIRED WHERE TRANSFER IS EXEMPT FROM *AD VALOREM* STAMP DUTY AS BELOW THRESHOLD

[1] I/We certify that the transaction effected by this instrument does not form part of a larger transaction or series of transactions in respect of which the amount or value, or aggregate amount or value, of the consideration exceeds £1,000.

[1] I/We confirm that [1]I/we have been duly authorised by the transferor to sign this certificate and that the facts of the transaction are within [1] my/our knowledge [2].

(1) Delete as appropriate

(2) Delete second sentence if certificate is given by transferor or his solicitor.

Signature(s)	*Description ("Transferor", "Solicitor", etc.)*
1. *D Doe*	TRANSFEROR
....	....
....	....

Date: 1 March 2008

Notes

(1) If the above certificate has been completed, this transfer does not need to be submitted to the Stamp Office but should be sent directly to the Company or its Registrars.

(2) If the above certificate is not completed, this transfer must be submitted to the Stamp Office and duly stamped.

[Form Conveyancing 40. This form is the copyright of Oyez Forms Publishing and is reproduced here with their permission.]

Form of Letter of Request

LETTER OF REQUEST	

above this line for Registrar's use only

REQUEST BY EXECUTORS OR ADMINISTRATORS OF A DECEASED HOLDER TO BE PLACED ON THE REGISTER AS HOLDERS IN THEIR OWN RIGHT

	TO THE DIRECTORS OF	
Full name of Undertaking.	KRANSTEIN SECURITIES	
* Full description of Security *(see note below)*.	30,000 x £1 ORDINARY SHARES	
Number or amount of Shares, Stock or other Security and, in figures column only, number and denomination of units, if any.	WORDS THIRTY THOUSAND	FIGURES 30,000 (units of £ 1)

Full name of Deceased   JOHN EDWARD DOE

I/We, the undersigned, being the personal representative(s) of the above-named deceased, hereby request you to register me/us in the books of the Company as the holder(s) of the above-mentioned Stock/Shares now registered in the name of the said deceased.

DATED this   1st   day of   MARCH   2008
Signature(s) of personal representative(s)

P Doe
....
....

PLEASE COMPLETE IN TYPEWRITING OR IN BLOCK CAPITALS Full name(s) and full postal address(es) (including postcodes) of the Personal Representative(s) in the order in which they are to be registered. Please state title, if any, or whether Mr, Mrs or Miss	PAUL MICHAEL DOE 4 THE CRESCENT ANYTOWN LOAMSHIRE A21 2XY MR

IF AN ACCOUNT ALREADY EXISTS IN THE ABOVE NAME(S) IN THE SAME ORDER THE ABOVE-MENTIONED HOLDING WILL BE ADDED TO THAT ACCOUNT, UNLESS INSTRUCTIONS ARE GIVEN TO THE CONTRARY.

The Certificate(s) in the name of the deceased if not already with the Company's Registrars must accompany this form. No stamp duty is payable on this form in the case of a company registered in England; in the case of a company registered in Scotland, stamp duty may be payable * A separate Letter of Request should be used for each class of security.	Stamp or name and address of person lodging this form

This form must be returned to:
The Registrar
.... (Name of Company)
.... (Address)
....
....

[Form Conveyancing 41A. This form is the copyright of Oyez Forms Publishing and is reproduced here with their permission.]

Bank and Building Society Accounts

If the deceased person had a bank account, a building society account, or both, in his or her sole name, all the personal representative needs to do is produce the grant of representation to the bank or building society. The grant is sufficient authority for the bank or building society to pay the funds to the personal representative, who holds the money until the time comes to pass it on.

If an account was in the joint names of a husband and wife or civil partners, it is generally accepted that the money belongs to them in equal shares even though only one of them may have been the only contributor, or may have contributed more than the other.

But this may not be so where the account holders were not married to, or partners of, each other; here the shares must be agreed between the personal representative and the survivor. If agreement cannot be reached it may be necessary to investigate how the account was funded. Obviously, if one person put in more than the other, that person would be entitled to the greater share. If agreement between the surviving account holder and the beneficiaries cannot be reached, the personal representative has to make a final decision. The risk is that the survivor of the joint account holders may disagree with the decision, and may sue the estate for what he or she considers appropriate. This would make for many difficulties – faced with the prospect of a legal action, the personal representative should consider seeking advice from a solicitor.

Assurance Policies

The benefits of assurances on the life of the deceased may be payable after death in a variety of ways. If a policy was in favour of a nominated beneficiary, the insurers usually pay the sum assured direct to that beneficiary on production of the death certificate, and will not need to see the grant of representation before paying. Similarly, if the policy provided for the payment of an annuity to a named beneficiary then, on acceptance of proof of death, the nominated beneficiary receives the annuity. There are no hard and fast rules and companies vary in their policies. The company will tell you if they wish to see the grant before paying out, and of course they are quite entitled to make such a requirement.

But if the sum assured and any profits form part of the estate, insurers may need to see the grant of representation before they make any payment. If so, a copy of the grant should be sent to them with a request for payment to the personal representative. Again, the proceeds should stay in the estate bank account for the time being.

Premium Bonds

If they are not cashed, premium bonds in the deceased's name remain eligible to be included in all prize draws for twelve months from the end of the month in which the deceased died. For example, if the deceased died on 8 April 2008, the premium bonds would remain in the draw until 30 April 2009 if not cashed before then. At the end of this time, they have to be cashed. Any prizes won after the date of death are part of the estate.

Premium bonds cannot be transferred from one person to another. So if there is a gift of premium bonds in a will, the bonds must be cashed and a sum of money equal to their value given instead. The beneficiary can then buy new bonds. Otherwise, the bonds should be cashed and the money paid into the estate bank account.

To cash the bonds, you need an encashment form, which can be obtained from the Controller, Premium Bonds, National Savings and Investments, Blackpool FY3 9YP, or downloaded at www.nsandi.com. The form should be completed and returned to the address given on the form. You will need the premium bonds themselves and the deceased's bond holder's card. National Savings and Investments may also ask for a copy of the grant of representation.

Other National Savings

The procedure for cashing any national savings certificates or income bonds is the same as for premium bonds, except that here you need to contact National Savings and Investments, Durham DH99 1NS. You may already have been in touch with this office before you applied for the grant of representation to ask for a valuation, which would have been needed when completing Form IHT205.

As mentioned earlier (see page 59), the deceased may have made arrangements with National Savings and Investments for some or all of his or her savings certificates to pass to a named person after death. If so, the Controller of National Savings and Investments will tell you. The nominated certificates pass to the named person and do not have to be dealt with by the personal representative.

Savings certificates differ from premium bonds in that it is possible, subject to certain conditions, to transfer savings certificates to another person. If there is a gift of savings certificates in the will, it may be possible to transfer them to the beneficiary. If there was no such gift, they must be cashed and the proceeds form part of the residue of the estate.

Forms to transfer or cash savings certificates are obtainable on request from the National Savings Office in Durham or may be downloaded at www.nsandi.com.

When considering whether to cash savings certificates, it should be borne in mind that there may be more money for the estate if certificates which have not been held for their full terms are allowed to mature. The Controller will, on request, provide information about how much money would be produced and when. Always consider the advice before acting. It is your responsibility to maximise the estate. You may also need to advise the beneficiaries as they may wish to realise their benefit immediately rather than wait to acquire a greater benefit, or *vice versa*.

The Liabilities

We turn now to the liabilities, including the debts, of the estate. All these must be agreed and settled.

Inheritance Claims

Certain people may apply to a court if they consider that what they receive under a deceased's will or intestacy is not the appropriate provision which should have been made for them. The application would be for an order that more be provided out of the deceased's estate. These applications would be made not to the probate registry, but, usually, to a county court. They are made under the Inheritance (Provision for Family and Dependants) Act 1975. The people who may make an application are set out in section 1 of the Act:

(a) the spouse or civil partner of the deceased who has not remarried;

(b) a former spouse or civil partner of the deceased who has not subsequently remarried or formed another civil partnership;

(c) where the deceased died after 1 January 1996, any person who, for a period of two years ending with the date of death, was living with the deceased in the same household as husband or wife or civil partner;

(d) a child of the deceased;

(e) a person who is not a child of the deceased, but who was, in the context of any marriage or civil partnership to which the deceased was at any time a party, treated by the deceased as a child of his or her family in relation to that marriage or civil partnership;

(f) any other person who, immediately before the death of the deceased, was being maintained, either wholly or partly, by the deceased.

An application under the Act must be made within six months of the date the grant of representation is issued. An application can be made later than this only if there are very special reasons. The court considering the application may make a variety of orders, including orders for periodical payments, for lump sum payments and for property to be transferred.

If there is any possibility of a claim against the estate, no assets should be distributed until six months have elapsed from the date of the issue of the grant of representation. If a claim is made, the estate must not be distributed until the claim has been finally determined by the court. If there is a claim, the personal representative may well wish to have advice from a solicitor.

Often a person wishing to make a claim will enter a "standing search" in the probate registry so that, on issue, a copy of the grant is sent to that person. The claimant then knows how long he or she has to make a claim.

Income Tax

The personal representative has to consider income tax from two points of view – first, there may be tax outstanding on income which the deceased received before he died; and second, income tax may be due on money received by the estate after death.

The deceased may have had an accountant to deal with his tax affairs; if so, the personal representative should get in touch with him or her. It may be advisable to allow that accountant to continue to act and to deal with tax matters up to (and, if so required, after) the date of death. This is a matter for you as personal representative.

If no accountant will be acting, it is necessary to locate the tax office which dealt with the deceased's tax affairs. If the address cannot be found in the deceased's personal papers, inquire at the tax office most convenient to you. It will help if you have the deceased's National Insurance number, which you may find in the personal papers, or you may be able to trace it by contacting the deceased's doctor, employer, or company which paid his or her pension.

Sometimes, if there is only a small amount of tax outstanding, the Inspector of Taxes may waive it, but this is a decision for the tax office, which must be contacted and given the details.

Income tax for the tax year 2007/2008 is 10 per cent on the first £2,230 of income and 22 per cent after that; if income exceeds £34,600, the 40 per cent higher rate applies. These personal allowances are amended in the budget proposals to be enacted in the Finance Act 2008, expected to come into force in August 2008. The new provisions remove the 10 per cent band and introduce a new band of 20 per cent on income up to £36,000, with the 40 per cent rate applying to all income above £36,000. In fact, because of the way budget proposals are now brought into force, these provisions already apply. The usual allowances, such as the personal allowance, which reduce the amount payable, apply to income received before the date of death, but there are no allowances against income received by the estate after death (i.e., there is no personal allowance available on income received after death).

Capital Gains Tax

Capital gains tax is levied when goods or other assets are sold for more than they cost. There is a capital gains tax annual exempt amount, of £9,600 for the tax year 2008/09, for individuals, personal representatives of deceased persons and trustees of certain settlements for the disabled. Every husband, wife, civil partner and child has his or her own £9,600 annual exempt amount. Certain items are exempt; these include the family home, motor cars, life assurance policies and military medals or decorations. Government stocks are also exempt from capital gains tax.

As with income tax, the personal representative must make sure that all capital gains tax due is paid; the tax may arise by reason of gains made by the deceased before the date of death, or it may be that a gain is made by the estate after death. As before, this is a matter of locating and contacting the deceased's tax office.

The annual exemption, of £9,600 a year from 6 April 2008, can be claimed by the personal representatives for the estate. If it seems likely that capital gains tax may be due, it may be wise to ask for advice from a stock broker, accountant or other financial adviser.

If shares or other items are sold by the personal representative as part of the administration of the estate, and a taxable gain is made, the personal representative must account to HM Revenue and Customs and the estate must pay the tax. The beneficiary who later receives the proceeds of sale is not responsible for it.

If assets are sold at a profit by the personal representative during the period of administration, it makes no difference to the inheritance tax position; no additional inheritance tax is payable on the increased value of the estate. On the other hand, if assets are sold within one year of the date of death at an overall loss (that is, a loss on all stocks and shareholdings), it is possible to claim a refund of inheritance tax.

Those who inherit the property in question acquire it at the probate value, that is, at the value at the date of death. If they later sell the property, any capital gains tax payable by them will be calculated on the difference between the value at the date of death (the probate value) and the price at which they sell.

Inheritance Tax
We have already dealt at length with inheritance tax in Chapters 4 and 5. In Chapter 8, we explain how to obtain final clearance from HM Revenue and Customs that all tax has been paid.

Other Debts
In Chapter 3, we mentioned the other debts – household bills and so on. By the time the grant has been issued, you should have a fairly clear picture of these, but if any details are outstanding, they should be chased up.

Chapter 8

Distributing the Estate

When you are sure you have collected together all the estate's assets and are aware of all the debts, you are almost ready to distribute the estate.

Instrument of Variation

If they wish, beneficiaries may vary the terms of the will or the intestacy provisions. This may be done so as to reduce the amount of inheritance tax payable, but may also be done when a beneficiary simply wishes to pass his benefit on to another person. This requires the completion of an "instrument of variation", more usually referred to as a deed of variation, within two years of death. There are various requirements to be met and anyone considering making a variation would be well advised to take legal advice.

Clearing the Debts and Liabilities

Before beginning the distribution, you must be sure there is no claim under the Inheritance Act (see pages 132–133).

Likewise, you must be certain that any income tax, capital gains tax or inheritance tax has been paid in full. You should obtain written confirmation from HM Revenue and Customs either that tax is not due, or that any tax due has been paid. For income tax and capital gains tax, this is simply a matter of writing to the Inspector of Taxes and asking for confirmation.

Clearance in respect of inheritance tax is obtained when HM Revenue and Customs returns Form D18 to the probate registry (see page 114). If, though, more assets or liabilities have come to light during the administration, perhaps bringing the estate up to a value which makes an inheritance tax account (Form IHT 200; see page 81) necessary, or meaning that more tax is payable, you should contact HM Revenue and Customs who will supply the appropriate forms.

You should now pay all the other debts of the estate (including the funeral account if it has not already been settled), from the cash in the estate account. Likewise, you can reimburse yourself from the estate account for the expenses of the administration – these include the costs of postage, telephone calls, valuation fees and so on. All these liabilities should be paid, and careful records kept, before final distribution. It may be prudent to send details of your expenditure to those entitled to the residue of the estate for their approval; after all, the expenses do come out of the residue of the estate. If you used a professional person in the administration – a stockbroker, for example – that person's fees must now be paid if they were not deducted from the proceeds of the sale.

The Estate Account

Before distributing the estate it is wise to prepare an account, ensuring that all debts and liabilities are included. An example of an estate account is set out on pages 148–149. Accuracy is essential since it would clearly be difficult to get money back if too much is paid out because of an error in calculating the total net estate or in dividing it up.

Interim Payments

Specific gifts in the will of items such as paintings or ornaments should be made as soon as possible. This eases the burden of administration in that the estate is disposed of to the beneficiaries quickly; and it reduces the value of the estate which needs to be insured. Specific legacies should also be paid as soon as conveniently possible. If possible, residuary legatees may be paid part of what is to come to them even before the liabilities have been calculated exactly. But extreme care is needed to ensure the estate will have enough left to meet all its liabilities when they are finally known. See also the paragraph on insufficient estate, on page 146.

Time Limits

It is generally accepted that the executor(s) or administrator(s) should gather in the assets and clear all the liabilities within one year of the date of death. This is often referred to as the "executor's year" or the "administrator's year". Indeed there is a statutory provision for this period, in section 44 of the Administration of Estates Act 1925.

The personal representative (the executor or administrator) is therefore not obliged to distribute the estate until one year from the date of death, but may do so earlier if everything is in order.

Any beneficiary may require the personal representative to make an inventory and account of the estate. A court would not usually order this before the expiry of the year, although it is possible to apply for such an order before the year has elapsed. Any legacy unpaid one year after the date of death carries interest, currently at six per cent a year, which accrues from the year end to the date of payment. As mentioned above, it may be wise to pay legacies as soon as sufficient funds are available. This avoids the risk of having to pay interest, which would come from the residue of the estate. If legacies are paid late, those entitled to the residue are doubly prejudiced by the delay – not only do they wait longer to receive their share, but the benefit is reduced by the interest which has had to be paid.

Distribution under a Will

Where the deceased left a will, the estate is distributed in accordance with the gifts contained in the will. As has been said before, legacies of money should be paid, and items of personal property (paintings or silverware, for example) should be handed over to the intended beneficiaries as soon as possible. This lessens the possibility of interest becoming due on an unpaid legacy, and reduces the cost of insuring the gift of personal property until released.

Items of a personal nature which are not specifically given by a will may be accepted by a legatee in place of, or towards payment of, his or her legacy. Sometimes a will provides for the executor to make a decision about the value of such items, but if there is no such provision and the value is not agreed between the specific legatee and the residuary legatee, the items will probably have to be sold.

A receipt for the money or goods should be obtained from the beneficiaries, and the fact that the gift has been handed over should be shown in the estate account. An example of a receipt is as follows:

"Received from ... [the sum of £1,000] or [a collection of china-faced dolls] from the estate of ... deceased. (Signature and date)."

Gifts of real property (a house or land) should likewise be put into effect. Forms to transfer land are available from law stationers, but the personal representative may prefer, and would be well-advised, to use the services of a solicitor or licensed conveyancer, especially if there is any doubt about the shares of tenants in common (see pages 53–54). If property is not correctly transferred, there will almost certainly be problems next time it comes to be sold.

When the specific gifts and legacies have been made, the residue of the estate can be determined and transferred to the residuary beneficiaries.

If the estate is not fully disposed of by the will, for example where there is no gift of residue, or the residuary beneficiaries have died (see page 145), that part of the estate which is not disposed of is distributed in accordance with the intestacy rules, and those most closely related to the deceased share the undisposed of estate as if there was no will; see below.

Distribution on Intestacy

The law provides rules to work out who is to inherit, and who is entitled to apply for a grant, if a person dies without leaving a valid will. These rules are explained next.

The figures in (a) and (b) below apply when death was on or after 1 December 1993. The figures have not been increased since that date; lower figures applied before that date.

We have already noted that "issue" means children and grandchildren. "Children" includes illegitimate children and children adopted by the deceased. We use the words "brother" and "sister" to mean brothers and sisters who have the same mother and father, that is, they are "of the whole blood", except where half brothers and half sisters are specifically mentioned. Half brothers and half sisters are those with only one parent in common. Finally, uncles and aunts means full uncles and aunts unless half uncles and aunts are specifically referred to. To qualify as an uncle or aunt, a person must have been a brother or sister (whole or half blood) of a parent of the deceased.

From 1 July 1996, the surviving spouse must survive by at least twenty-eight days to acquire a beneficial interest. The twenty-eight day survival period applies to civil partners from 5 December 2005.

(a)   Intestate Leaves a Spouse or Civil Partner and Issue
If the intestate person leaves a spouse or civil partner and issue, and the net estate is worth £125,000 or less, the surviving spouse or civil partner is entitled to the grant of representation and inherits the entire estate.

If the net estate is worth more than £125,000, again the surviving spouse or civil partner is entitled to the grant. The spouse or civil partner also receives:

- £125,000 (this is often called the "statutory legacy");
- interest on the above amount at six per cent from the date of death until payment;
- the personal chattels (see page 55); and
- a life interest in half the rest of the property. This means that the spouse or civil partner has the benefit of this property until he or she dies, when it passes to the children of the intestate.

The other half of the remainder passes to the children immediately. For example, if the estate is worth £200,000, the wife or civil partner receives £125,000, plus income on £37,500 (that is, half of the remaining £75,000) for her life; after his/her death the £37,500 capital passes to the children. The children share the other £37,500 equally.

(b)   Intestate Leaves a Spouse or Civil Partner but no Issue
Where the deceased person leaves a spouse or civil partner, but no issue, if the net estate is worth £200,000 or less, the spouse or civil partner receives it all, and is the person entitled to the grant of representation.

If the estate is worth more than £200,000, the spouse or civil partner receives:

- a statutory legacy of £200,000;
- interest on the above amount at six per cent from the date of death until payment;

- the personal chattels (see page 55); and
- half the remaining property.

The other half of the remaining property goes to any surviving parent of the intestate, in equal shares if both parents survive. If both the intestate's parents are dead, this half is shared equally between brothers and sisters; if any brother or sister has died, the share he or she would have had goes to their children or grandchildren.

If the intestate person left a spouse or civil partner but no issue, no parent, no brother or sister and no nephews, nieces, great nephews or great nieces, the surviving spouse or civil partner inherits the entire estate no matter the size.

(c)   Intestate Leaves Issue but no Surviving Spouse or Civil Partner

Where the intestate leaves issue, but no surviving spouse or civil partner, those who have the right to apply for the grant are the children and grandchildren (that is, grandchildren whose parent, the child of the intestate, died before the intestate). Those who reach the age of eighteen or marry under the age of eighteen share the estate equally. If any of the intestate's children or grandchildren has already died, their share goes to their children or grandchildren.

(d)   Intestate Leaves One or Both Parents but no Spouse or Civil Partner or Issue

If the deceased person leaves a parent, but no spouse or civil partner, and no issue, the parent may apply for the grant and receives the entire estate. If both parents survive, they are equally entitled to the grant and share the estate equally.

(e)   Intestate Leaves Brother(s)/Sister(s), but no Spouse or Civil Partner, Issue or Parent

Where the intestate leaves brother(s) and/or sister(s), but no spouse or civil partner, no issue and no parent, the brother(s) and/or sister (s) share the estate equally and are equally entitled to the grant of representation. If any of the intestate's brothers or sisters has already died, their share goes to their issue.

(f)   Intestate Leaves only Half Brothers/Sisters or their Issue

Where none of those mentioned in (e) above survives, but there are half brothers or half sisters or both, they share the estate. Again, if any of them has already died, their share goes to their issue. The people entitled to share the estate are all equally entitled to apply for the grant.

(g) Intestate Leaves only Grandparents

Where the intestate leaves none of the relatives mentioned in (e) and (f), but one or more of his or her grandparents survives, then the grandparents share the estate and are equally entitled to the grant.

(h) Intestate Leaves only Uncles, Aunts or Cousins

Where none of those in (e), (f) and (g) are left, but there are uncles and aunts, the uncles and aunts share the estate. If any uncle or aunt died before the intestate, their share passes on to their issue. Again, the uncles and aunts who share the estate may apply for the grant.

(i) Intestate Leaves only Half Uncles and Half Aunts or Half Cousins

If none of those mentioned above survives, but the intestate leaves half uncles, half aunts or both, they share the estate and are equally entitled to apply for the grant. If any of them died before the intestate, the shares they would have received go instead to their children or grandchildren.

(j) No Surviving Relative

If the intestate person leaves no relatives, the estate goes to the Crown or to a creditor. Where there is no blood relative of the deceased, or if those entitled to the estate renounce their right to the grant, then a creditor may apply. The creditor deducts the debt from the estate, but must pay over the balance to the person(s) entitled to benefit in accordance with the rules described above. If there is no person to benefit and no creditor, the Treasury Solicitor takes the grant for the Crown; the estate passes to the Crown as "bona vacantia".

Beneficiaries

Minors

Where a person who is to benefit under either a will or an intestacy is under eighteen, the gift cannot be made until the young person (the minor) reaches full age. Until then, the gift of money or property is managed by trustees. There should always be more than one trustee. Sometimes, those appointed executors are also appointed trustees and may themselves take charge of the "trust fund". If not, trustees must be appointed to receive the gift and invest it. When the beneficiary reaches eighteen, the benefit may be transferred to him or her.

Will trusts may make special provision for advancing money, either income or capital, from the trust to the minor. Great care must be taken by the trustees to deal with the trust correctly.

Acting as a trustee is onerous, involving many responsibilities, including making investment decisions and accounting to HM Revenue and Customs. It is usual for the executor and/or administrator, as the "personal representative", to be a trustee, but there are no hard and fast rules. If the gift is large it may be preferable to have a solicitor or accountant as a co-trustee. It is beyond the scope of this book to examine the subject in any detail. If a trust arises, it would almost certainly be necessary to obtain legal advice.

Children of the Deceased
Legitimate and illegitimate children benefit equally from the estates of their intestate parents. Illegitimacy no longer has any significance for these purposes.

Children who were legally adopted by the deceased have the same status as natural children and are equally entitled to benefit from the estate.

On the other hand, a natural child of the deceased who was adopted by someone else has no right to share in the estate of an intestate deceased. Instead, the child is entitled to inherit from the adopters. On adoption, a child ceases to be the child of his or her natural parents and becomes the child of the adopters.

The former legal requirement concerning what were known as "advancements" has now been abolished. This applied where more than one child stood to inherit from a parent, and property had been "advanced" – given to one of the children – before the parent dies. If the parent died intestate, and if there was nothing to suggest that the parent intended to favour the child to whom the property was advanced at the expense of the other child or children, then the value advanced had to be taken into account when calculating how the estate was to be divided.

Missing Beneficiaries

Sometimes a person who is to receive a gift under a will or to share in an intestacy cannot immediately be traced. The personal representative must do all he or she sensibly can to find the beneficiary, but must not incur unreasonable expenses in trying to do so.

An obvious step is to contact those now living at the beneficiary's last known address, who may have a forwarding address or may know where the beneficiary moved. The electoral roll or the council tax register may help; so too may the telephone directory.

The Benefits Agency, through its records office in Newcastle-upon-Tyne, may be able to help. The Agency will not disclose a person's address, but will forward a stamped envelope containing a letter requesting the beneficiary to contact the personal representative.

It is also possible to place an advertisement, either in a local newspaper circulating in the area where you believe the beneficiary lives, or in a national newspaper, but this can be expensive. The *News of the World* is the best known newspaper for advertising for missing beneficiaries, but it is extremely expensive.

If all attempts to trace the beneficiary fail, you may pay the gift into court. This is done by applying to the Court Funds Office, Royal Courts of Justice, Strand, London WC2A 2LL. They will give information about the procedure.

Alternatively, you may buy a "missing beneficiary's indemnity" from an insurance company. Most of the larger insurance companies offer such policies. You pay a single premium from the estate's funds and you may then distribute the estate among the known beneficiaries. If the missing person later claims the gift, the insurance company pays. The Chancery Division of the High Court, in a recent case, advocated this course in preference to paying the money into court.

A further alternative is to apply to the Chancery Court for a distribution order (sometimes referred to as a "Benjamin Order" after the name of the case on which the order was based). The application will be for an order for distribution to the known beneficiaries only. This form of application is usually made when the estate is large and can bear the costs of an application to the High Court.

Where a Gift Cannot be Made

Where a will contains a gift to a beneficiary and the beneficiary dies before the deceased, the gift lapses – that is, it does not take effect. Instead, it falls back into the residuary estate, unless the will specifically provides for it to go elsewhere in these circumstances – commonly called "a gift over". For example, if a will provides for a gift of £1,000 to A, and A dies before the deceased, the gift lapses, but if the will provides for the gift to pass to B if A predeceases, then B receives the £1,000.

In the same way, a gift of the residue of the estate to be divided equally between, say, three people, cannot be shared by just two of them if the third dies before the testator, unless the will provided for this to happen. The predeceasing beneficiary's share is instead undisposed of, and is distributed according to the intestacy rules (see page 139).

Where a will contains a gift or legacy to a beneficiary who survives the deceased, but dies before receiving the gift or legacy, the gift remains with the beneficiary and forms part of his or her estate to be distributed in accordance with his or her will or intestacy. If the gift is contingent upon the beneficiary surviving for a prescribed period before the gift is effective then obviously the beneficiary must survive by the requisite period to receive the gift. In the absence of a "gift over" to someone else, the share falls into the residue if the beneficiary fails to survive the prescribed period.

We have already mentioned (see page 10) that there is special legal provision (in section 33 of the Wills Act 1837) which applies where a will contains a gift to a child or grandchild. If the child or grandchild dies before the testator, leaving a child or children of his or her own who do survive the testator, then the gift takes effect as a gift to that child or children, as long as there is nothing else in the will to prevent this from happening. For example, Albert leaves £10,000 by will to his son, Brian, but does not say what is to happen if Brian dies first. Brian has a son of his own, Charles. Brian does die before Albert, but Charles survives both his father and his grandfather. The gift to Brian is saved and, instead of going back into the residuary estate, it becomes a gift to Charles.

Insufficient Funds to Make the Gift

Where the money left in the estate after paying all the debts and expenses is insufficient to pay the legacies, the legacies "abate" – that is, they are reduced in equal proportions. For example, if there are bequests of £1,000 and £500 and a gift of residue, but the net estate amounts to £750 only, the first bequest becomes £500 and the second £250, and there is no residue left to distribute. What is more, some legacies abate before others; for example, gifts of money abate before gifts of a specific nature (such as "my books").

If there is a possibility that the net estate may be insufficient to meet the bequests, great care is needed before anything is given out. If one legacy is paid in full, the other beneficiaries may be able to argue that this indicates there were sufficient funds to pay all the legacies in full; they may even be able to make out a case that the personal representative is at fault and should make good the shortfall himself or herself. On the other hand, if a legacy was paid in full in these circumstances by mistake, and any subsequent dispute reaches a court, the court could compel the recipient to repay part of the money.

Where the deceased died intestate and the estate is divided between those known to be entitled, but later another person with an equal right makes a claim, a court might order those among whom the estate was divided to repay part of what they received.

It is clearly wise, before making any distribution, to ensure that there is sufficient in the net estate to meet the specific bequests, and that all those with a right to a share are known to the personal representative, even if this means delaying the distribution.

Interest

Any legacy directed by a will to be paid immediately on death carries interest, from the date of death until payment, at, currently, six per cent. Interest at the same rate becomes payable on other legacies which are unpaid after one year from the date of death. The amount of any such interest is deducted from the residue of the estate before payment to the residuary beneficiaries.

We have already noted (see page 140) that where a spouse or civil partner survives an intestate, interest, again at six per cent, is payable on the statutory legacy. It accrues from the date of death until the legacy is paid.

Gifts to Executors

If a will contains a gift to an executor, and the gift is conditional on the executor's accepting the appointment as executor, the gift will be void if the person named does not act as executor. Instead, it falls back into the residuary estate.

A personal representative, whether executor or administrator, must not make any profit from acting as such in the administration of the estate. Although he or she may recover from the estate the expenses of postage, telephone calls and so on, there can be no charge for performing the administration. The only exception to this is, obviously, where a solicitor, accountant or bank is appointed executor and there is a clause in the will allowing the appointee to charge for professional services. If there is no "charging clause" in the will, a professional administrator may still act, but the professional person's terms of business must be approved first, and the fees charged must be agreed by the residuary beneficiaries before distribution.

Payment

When you are quite satisfied about the final value of the estate after paying all the debts, the legacies in the will may be paid and the residuary estate passed to the residuary legatee, or divided among the residuary legatees if there is more than one. Each payment made should be accompanied by a request for a receipt. A copy of the estate account should also be sent to the residuary beneficiaries. It may be wise, if there is any chance the residuary beneficiaries may question their shares, to send a copy of the account to them for their approval before distributing any of the estate.

Where any payments include interest, a statement setting out the principal and the interest should be prepared. If any tax has been deducted from the payment, a tax deduction certificate should be supplied by the personal representative. These forms of certificate (Form R185E) are obtainable from HM Revenue and Customs.

Where the deceased died intestate the net estate is apportioned in accordance with the rules described on pages 139–142.

When distribution is complete the estate account should have a zero balance and it may be closed. Administration has now finished, as have your duties to the deceased's estate.

The Estate Account

Set out below is an example of an estate account. In the first part, the Capital Account, the money received from the sale of assets is itemised, and money spent during the administration is set out. The Income Account shows the money earned by the estate during the period of the administration, leaving a net estate of £330,732. The Distribution Account shows exactly what has been done with the money.

Specimen Estate Account

In the Estate of John Edward Doe, Deceased
Covering the period from ... to ...

1. CAPITAL ACCOUNT

Assets at the date of death (13.10.07)	*Debit*	*Credit*

Receipts

Property, 12 Acacia Avenue, Middlemarch		£340,000
Stocks and shares:		
Superprofits plc, 1,000 ordinary shares		£15,000
Hyperion Stores plc, 1,000 ordinary shares		£15,000
International Shipping, 2,000 ordinary shares		£40,000
Life assurance policy		£25,000
Building Society A/C (Kingdom Building Society)		£7,500
Bank A/C (Black Eagle Bank)		£1,400
Bank A/C (Kaplan's Bank) (Current A/C)		£1,100
Bank A/C (Kaplan's Bank) (Deposit A/C)		£8,000
National Savings		£500
Pension (employer)		£250
Pension (State)		£150
Income tax refund		£80
Cash		£25
TOTAL (the gross estate)		**£454,005**

Payments made

Repayment of mortgage	£100,000	
Funeral account	£900	
Outstanding debts (schedule annexed)	£1,100	
Inheritance tax	£20,802	
Probate fees	£96	
Valuation fees	£400	
Administrator's/executor's expenses	£430	
TOTAL	**£123,728**	

Receipts less payments carried forward to
distribution A/C: ....

2. INCOME ACCOUNT

Stocks and shares

Gain in value between date of death
and sale/transfer.. £250
Interest/dividends received.. £75
Bank A/C interest received £15
Building society A/C interest received.. £115
TOTAL **£455**

Total to distribution A/C (the net estate) **£330,732**

3. DISTRIBUTION ACCOUNT

Specific legacies	Mr A Early	(notice of gift) (value £50.00)
	Mrs V Butler	(notice of gift) (value £100.00)
	Mrs A Phillip	(notice of gift) (value £150.00)
Pecuniary legacies	Mrs Trussler	Cash.................... (£1,000.00)
	Mrs R Jones	Cash.................... (£1,000.00)
	Mrs K Anderton	Cash.................... (£1,000.00)
	Mrs M Warren	Cash....................(£2,000.00)
Residuary estate	Mrs H Brand (one quarter)................ £81,358
	Mr L Brabant (one quarter)..................£81,358
	Mrs K Seabrook (one quarter)............. £81,358
	Mrs M Kingdom (one quarter)........ £81,358
	£330,732

Intestacy and the Family Home

We have already noted that one of the harshest consequences of not making a will is that a spouse or civil partner may be at risk of having to leave the family home.

The way an intestate's estate is shared may be varied where the surviving spouse's statutory legacy is less than the value of the house in which the deceased and the surviving spouse or civil partner lived. Under the present provisions, if the deceased leaves a spouse and children, the surviving spouse or civil partner receives £125,000; interest on that to the date of payment; the personal effects; and a life interest in one half of the remainder. Thus, if the estate is worth £200,000, the spouse or civil partner receives

£125,000 plus the income from £37,500 for his or her life. The remaining £37,500 passes to the children in equal shares. Suppose the house was owned by the deceased alone, and not by the spouses or civil partners as joint tenants so as to pass to the survivor on the death of one of them. It is valued at, say, £150,000. There is an excess of £25,000 in the value of the house over the value to which the surviving spouse or civil partner is entitled. The surviving spouse or civil partner may therefore have to pay the difference in value, or even sell the house to make up the difference.

The problem may be resolved with the agreement of the deceased's children (as long as they are not minors), by transferring the property to the children with a provision for the surviving parent to remain living there; or by transferring the property into the names of the surviving parent and the children as beneficial joint tenants or as tenants in common in the relevant shares. This can be complicated, and it would probably be necessary to have the help of a solicitor to put a plan like this into effect.

Redeeming a Life Interest

A surviving spouse or civil partner entitled to a life interest in one half of the estate over the statutory legacy (as described on page 140) may decide to "redeem" that life interest. The effect is that the remaining property is divided among the spouse or civil partner and the children immediately, so there is no life interest. This has the attraction of simplicity. Again, there is a particular procedure to be followed, and we recommend you consult a solicitor if you think this course might be appropriate.

Appendix

List of Probate Registries, Sub-Registries and Offices

East

IPSWICH: Ground Floor, 8 Arcade Street, Ipswich IP1 1EJ. Telephone: (01473) 253 724.

Probate Offices: Chelmsford, Colchester.

NORWICH: Combined Court Building, The Law Courts, Bishopsgate, Norwich NR3 1UR. Telephone: (01603) 728 267.

Probate Offices: Lowestoft, Kings Lynn.

PETERBOROUGH: First Floor, Crown Buildings, Rivergate, Peterborough PE1 1EJ. Telephone: (01733) 562 802.

Probate Offices: Cambridge, King's Lynn.

LINCOLN: 360, High Street, Lincoln LN5 7PS. Telephone: (01522) 523 648.

Probate Office: Grimsby.

Midlands

BIRMINGHAM: The Priory Courts, 33 Bull Street, Birmingham B4 6DU. Telephone: (0121) 681 3400.

Probate Offices: Coventry, Kidderminster, Lichfield, Northampton, Wolverhampton.

LEICESTER: Crown Court Building, 90 Wellington Street, Leicester LE1 6HG. (0116) 285 3380.

Probate Offices: Bedford, Kettering.

NOTTINGHAM: Butt Dyke House, 33 Park Row, Nottingham NG1 6GR. Telephone: (0115) 941 4288.

Probate Offices: Derby, Mansfield.

STOKE-ON-TRENT: Combined Court Centre, Bethesda Street, Hanley, Stoke-on-Trent ST1 3BP. Telephone: (01782) 854 065.

Probate Offices: Crewe, Shrewsbury, Stafford.

North

LEEDS: Third Floor, Coronet House, Queen Street, Leeds LS1 2BA. Telephone: (0113) 386 3540.

Probate Offices: Bradford, Harrogate, Huddersfield, Wakefield.

SHEFFIELD: PO Box 832, The Law Courts, 50 West Bar, Sheffield S3 8YR. Telephone: (0114) 281 2596

Probate Offices: Chesterfield, Doncaster.

YORK: First Floor, Castle Chambers, Clifford Street, York YO1 9RG. Telephone: (01904) 666 777.

Probate Offices: Hull, Scarborough.

North East

CARLISLE: Courts of Justice, Earl Street, Carlisle, Cumbria CA1 1DJ. Telephone: (01228) 521 751.

Probate Office: Workington.

MIDDLESBROUGH; Teesside Combined Court Centre, Russell Street, Middlesbrough TS1 2AE. Telephone: (01642) 430 001.

Probate Offices: Darlington, Durham. Contact Newcastle District Probate Registry for opening hours.

NEWCASTLE: No. 1 Waterloo Square, Newcastle-upon-Tyne, NE1 4AL. Telephone: (0191) 211 2170.

Probate Offices: Morpeth, Sunderland, Darlington.

North West

CHESTER: Second Floor, Chester Civil Justice Centre, Trident House, Little St. John Street, Chester CH1 1RE. Telephone: (01244) 345 082.

Probate Offices: Rhyl, Wrexham.

LANCASTER: Mitre House, Church Street, Lancaster LA1 1HE. Telephone: (01524) 36625.

Probate Offices: Barrow, Blackpool, Preston, St. Helens.

LIVERPOOL: Queen Elizabeth II Law Courts, Derby Square, Liverpool L2 1XA. Telephone: (0151) 236 8264.

Probate Offices: St Helens, Southport, Wallasey.

MANCHESTER: Ground Floor, 1 Bridge Street West, PO Box 4240, Manchester M60 1WJ. Telephone: (0161) 240 5700.

Probate Offices: Bolton, Burnley, Nelson, Oldham, Stockport, Warrington, Wigan.

South

OXFORD: The Combined Court Building, St Aldates, Oxford OX1 1LY. Telephone: (01865) 793 050.

Probate Offices: Aylesbury, Banbury, High Wycombe, Reading, Slough, Swindon.

WINCHESTER: Fourth Floor, Cromwell House, Andover Road, Winchester SO23 7EW. Telephone: (01962) 897 029.

Probate Offices: Basingstoke, Bournemouth, Dorchester, Guildford, Newport Isle of Wight, Portsmouth, Salisbury, Southampton.

South East
BRIGHTON: William Street, Brighton BN2 2LG. Telephone: (01273) 573 510.
Probate Offices: Chichester, Crawley, Hastings, Horsham.
MAIDSTONE: The Law Courts, Barker Road, Maidstone ME16 8EQ. Telephone: (01622) 202 048.
Probate Offices: Canterbury, Chatham, Folkestone, Tunbridge Wells.

London
The Principal Registry: The Probate Department, First Avenue House, 42-49 High Holborn, London WC1V 6NP. Telephone: (020) 7947 6939.

South West
BODMIN: Market Street, Bodmin, Cornwall PL31 2JW. Telephone: (01208) 72279.
Probate Offices: Plymouth, Truro.
EXETER: Second Floor, Exeter Crown and County Courts, Southernhay Gardens, Exeter EX1 1UH. Telephone: (01392) 415 370.
Probate Offices: Barnstaple, Taunton, Torquay/Newton Abbot, Yeovil.

Wales
BANGOR: Council Offices, Ffordd Gwynedd, Bangor LL57 1DT. Telephone: (01248) 362 410.
Probate Offices: Rhyl, Wrexham.
CARMARTHEN: 14 King Street, Carmarthen SA31 1BL. Telephone: (01267) 242 560.
Probate Offices: Aberystwyth, Haverfordwest, Swansea.
CARDIFF: PO Box 474, 2 Park Street, Cardiff CF10 1TB. Telephone: (029) 2037 6479.
Probate Offices: Bridgend, Newport, Pontypridd.

West
BRISTOL: The Crescent Centre, Temple Back, Bristol BS1 6EP. Telephone: (0117) 927 3915.
Probate Offices: Bath, Taunton, Weston-super-Mare.
GLOUCESTER: Second Floor, Combined Court Building, Kimbrose Way, Gloucester GL1 2DG Telephone: (01452) 834 966.
Probate Offices: Cheltenham, Hereford, Worcester.

Glossary

Administering the estate: the process of gathering together all the estate assets, paying off the debts, and passing on the remainder to those entitled to it.

Administrator: the person who obtains letters of administration of the deceased's estate, the deceased having died intestate.

Assets: all the property in the estate; it includes both real and personal property.

Attestation clause: the formal part at the end of a will, where the person making the will and the witnesses sign, which confirms that all the formalities were complied with

Beneficiary: someone who receives a benefit – either real or personal property – under a will or intestacy.

Bequest: a gift of personal property.

Codicil: an "appendix" to a will, a further separate testamentary document, altering or adding provisions to a will. See page 28.

Devise: a gift of land or other real property.

Disposition: any kind of gift in a will disposing of property.

Distributing the estate: the process of handing over the deceased's property, after the debts have been paid, to those who inherit it.

Estate: used to describe all the assets which can be disposed of under the will or which pass under an intestacy. Jointly held assets which pass by survivorship automatically to the other joint owner and "nominated" assets (see page 59) do not form part of the estate.

Executor: a person appointed by the deceased in his or her will to deal with the estate after death.

Grant of representation: the document issued by the court giving legal recognition to the personal representative. They are called grants – because they are granted by the court – of probate (to the executor), or letters of administration (to a beneficiary under a will or intestacy).

Immovable: property which is fixed, used to describe houses or land.

Intestate: a person who dies without making a valid will.

Issue: children, grandchildren, great grandchildren and so on.

Joint assets: property owned by two or more people. They may own it as "joint tenants" or "tenants in common"; see page 53.

Legacy: a gift of personal property.

Minor: a child under the age of eighteen years.

Movable: property which is not fixed; assets which can be "moved" (such as cash in a bank account and shares).

Personal applicant: A person who applies for a grant of representation without instructing a solicitor.

Personal property: property other than freehold houses or land. The expression includes leasehold property. Sometimes called "personalty".

Personal representative: a person, either executor or administrator, who has been named in the grant of representation as the person authorised to deal with the deceased's estate.

Probate office: A satellite office of a probate registry where personal applicants are interviewed by appointment.

Probate registry: A branch of the Family Division of the High Court of Justice. It is the function of these offices to prove wills and issue grants of administration.

Real property: freehold houses or land (sometimes called "realty").

Registrar: A senior officer appointed by the Lord Chancellor as the judicial decision-maker in a probate registry.

Residue: The assets left in the estate after all the debts, liabilities and specific gifts have been paid.

Said: a term used in a will to refer back to something or someone mentioned earlier. For example, if you name Frederick Bloggs as an executor and then make a gift to him under the will, he should be referred to on the second occasion as "the said Frederick Bloggs". This ensures that there can be no confusion about the identity of the person or object referred to.

Specific gift: A gift in a will of a particular thing or things, such as "my collection of antique silverware".

Undisposed of estate: Property not given away by will; see page 15.

Index